Interviewing Right:
How Science Can Sharpen Your Interviewing Accuracy

George S. Hallenbeck Jr.
Robert W. Eichinger

Foreword by
Michael A. Campion
Krannert School of Management
Purdue University

Guest Contributors:

Michael A. Campion

Linda Hodge
Hodge & Associates

Marilyn Westmas
Berbee Information Networks

INTERVIEWING RIGHT:

How Science Can Sharpen Your Interviewing Accuracy

Published by Lominger International: A Korn/Ferry Company
Minneapolis, Minnesota 55416-2291
Tel. 952-345-3600 • Fax. 952-345-3601
www.lominger.com

ISBN: 1-933578-10-6
Lominger reorder part number: 41030

Interviewing Right: How Science Can Sharpen Your Interviewing Accuracy
1st Edition Printings:
version 06.1a 1st–10/06
version 06.1a 2nd–01/08
version 06.1a 3rd–01/10
version 06.1a 4th–06/10
version 06.1a 5th–10/11
version 06.1a 6th–05/12
version 06.1a 7th–11/12

ABOUT THE AUTHORS

George Hallenbeck is responsible for developing and managing Lominger International's INTERVIEW ARCHITECT® suite of products. Prior to joining Lominger, George spent eight years as a consultant specializing in executive assessment and has conducted hundreds of candidate interviews to assist clients with their hiring and promotion decisions. He also has extensive experience as an executive coach and has designed and implemented several training courses on leadership and interpersonal skills. He has an MS and PhD in industrial and organizational psychology from Colorado State University.

Bob Eichinger is President of Lominger International and, along with Mike Lombardo, co-creator of The LEADERSHIP ARCHITECT® suite of manager and executive development products and co-author of *The Leadership Machine*, a source book on developing people. Bob has over 40 years experience in management and executive development. He held executive development positions at PepsiCo and Pillsbury and has consulted with hundreds of organizations on succession planning and development. He has lectured extensively on the topic of executive and management development and has served on the Board of the Human Resource Planning Society, a professional association of people charged with the responsibility of management and executive development in their organizations. He has been a one-on-one feedback giver and coach from both inside and outside organizations. Bob has worked personally with over 1,000 managers and executives during his career. He has served on feedback teams within courses and off-sites in various organizations and public courses.

OUR CONTRIBUTORS

Michael A. Campion is a Professor of Management at Purdue University, where he has been a member of the faculty for the last 20 years. His previous industrial experience includes eight years at IBM and Weyerhaeuser Company. He has an MS and PhD in industrial and organizational psychology. He has 90 articles published in scientific and professional journals and has given nearly 180 presentations at professional meetings on topics such as interviewing, testing, job analysis, work design, teams, training, turnover, promotion, and motivation. He is among the 10 most published authors in the top journals in his field for the past two decades. He is past editor of *Personnel Psychology* (a scientific research journal) and past president of the Society of Industrial and Organizational Psychology. He is well-known for his research on structured interviewing, from his initial work in the 1980s up to his comprehensive reviews in recent years.

Linda Hodge is President of HODGE & ASSOCIATES, Inc., a leadership and organization development consulting firm. Her company specializes in designing and implementing selection and development processes and developing strategies for strengthening the talent bench. Linda has 20 years of business experience in manufacturing, retail, service, computer, and health care organizations, including three Fortune 500 companies. She is an Associate of Lominger International and a Master Certifier for the LEADERSHIP ARCHITECT® suite of products. In conjunction with Lominger founders Bob Eichinger and Mike Lombardo, Linda has helped develop several of Lominger's interviewing products. Linda holds a bachelor's degree in communication and psychology and a master's degree in clinical psychology from Ball State University.

Marilyn Westmas is Director of Organizational Development and Marketing Communications for Berbee Information Networks Corporation, a provider of a wide range of IT solutions. She has a long history of experience working in rapid growth, high-tech environments. Prior to joining Berbee in 2000, she held OD management roles at Rayovac Corporation (now Spectrum Brands) and Telephone and Data Systems. Marilyn has extensive experience with developing HR solutions using Lominger products and is a certified user of a number of tools in the LEADERSHIP ARCHITECT® suite. She has her bachelor's and master's degrees from the University of Wisconsin – Madison.

ACKNOWLEDGMENTS

We would like to take a moment to recognize the contributions of the many individuals who provided their time and expertise to make this book a reality. We could not have accomplished this without their efforts.

Our layout and design team of Lesley Kurke and Eric Ekstrand did their usual exemplary job of pulling together varying pieces of content and assembling it all into a cohesive and aesthetically pleasing whole. Extra thanks to Lesley for integrating information from multiple drafts and contributors and to Eric for an excellent cover art design and layout.

Bonnie Parks, our longtime editor, patiently combed through the many versions of the manuscript and made myriad helpful suggestions to sharpen our tone, clarity, and grammar. Her attention to detail and commitment to quality are greatly appreciated.

Guangrong Dai went above and beyond the call in responding to our many requests for up-to-date research information, often going to great lengths to quickly acquire key articles and track down a wide range of references.

An extra special thanks to our trio of guest contributors: Michael Campion, Linda Hodge, and Marilyn Westmas. They generously gave their time and considerable expertise to this project. We hope you enjoy their wisdom and insights and are able to put their ideas into practice during your own interview sessions.

Finally, we would like to thank our families for their patience, encouragement, and support as we worked through the long, sometimes difficult, but always rewarding, process of putting this book together.

INTERVIEWING RIGHT

TABLE OF CONTENTS

FOREWORD

Organizations cannot afford to make poor personnel selection decisions. Most businesses are in such competitive markets these days that every advantage (or disadvantage) counts. Each new hire or promotion affects productivity, quality, customer service, innovation, and safety, as well as job satisfaction, commitment, turnover, absenteeism, and labor relations. It is no wonder that virtually every list of company values, and most every executive speech, includes a statement about the importance of the employees to the success of the enterprise.

The payoff of a good hiring decision, or the cost of a poor one, is a matter of much debate. At a minimum, most researchers in human resources agree that the financial value of a hiring decision is related to the wages and benefits paid to the employee—on average, employees must be worth at least as much as they are paid, or the enterprise could not make a profit. If you accept that, then one way to get a handle on the financial importance of hiring decisions is to take the expected wages to be paid to the new hire plus benefits (usually another 25% to 40% of wages) and multiply it times the average number of years employees tend to stay in the organization. For example, if you hire administrative personnel who make $40,000 per year (or $50,000 with benefits) and the average employee stays 5 years, then you are making at least a $250,000 hiring decision. If you are hiring a manager who makes $80,000 per year (or $100,000 with benefits) and the average employee stays 10 years, then you are making a $1,000,000 hiring decision. Multiply this out times the number of hiring decisions a company makes in a year, and you can easily see the huge financial consequences.

One problem with making good hiring decisions is the statistical probabilities of it all. Consider the fact that most human attributes, from physical attributes like strength and dexterity, to personal attributes like intelligence and personality, are normally distributed (or nearly so) as demonstrated in the following "Normal Curve" (or "Bell Curve") that shows the number of people at each level of the attribute.

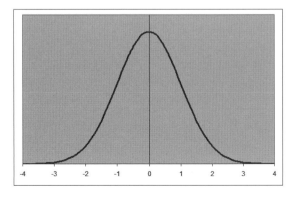

Job-related knowledge and skills are also distributed roughly as a normal curve. There are three implications of this:

1. There is a small number in the upper tail. There are very few superstars in the candidate pool. You must recruit, interview, and assess a lot of candidates to identify those few. These people can really give you a competitive advantage.

2. Most people are in the middle. With luck, most employees will be about average if you don't do anything special in hiring. Of course, hiring people in the middle may not give you a competitive advantage.

3. There are some poor performers out there in the lower tail. If hired, they will cause you most of your HR problems (e.g., managing poor performance, absenteeism, morale problems, turnover, etc.). You must have a good hiring process to avoid inadvertently hiring these people. If you do not have a good hiring process, then you are taking your chances.

So, how do you make good hiring decisions? Fortunately, there is a huge science behind personnel selection. It has been a primary topic of research for 100 years. There are tens of thousands of articles and books on the topic. There are so many studies on the topic, that there are now what we call "meta-analyses," which are statistical summaries of studies. Meta-analyses have shown that well-developed hiring tools can accurately identify the best candidates in nearly all jobs, occupations, and organizations.

Few research findings in the science of personnel selection are better supported than the finding that structured (planned, science-based) interviews are more valid than unstructured (informal, casual) interviews. There are hundreds of scientific articles and books on the topic. They are summarized in eight narrative reviews and seven meta-analytic reviews. Each one of these reviews has come to the same resounding conclusion—interviews should be planned for and structured.

So why is this finding the case? A fundamental scientific principle is that you cannot have validity (accuracy in picking the best future job performers) if you do not first have reliability. Reliability refers to the consistency, repeatability, and lack of error in measuring something. Traditional (informal, unplanned, casual) interviews are not very reliable. For example, different interviewers ask different questions and they evaluate the same information differently. How can they even begin to compare candidates?

So how do you get reliability or consistency? The answer is "standardization." There must be consistency, regularity, and equivalence across interviews in order for the interviews to measure anything well enough that they could possibly predict something else. In other words, how can an interview predict future job performance if it cannot measure candidate aptitude in a consistent manner?

The other part of the story is job relatedness. The interview questions must relate to the important skills and competencies required to do the job. The interview must not only measure things well, but it must measure things that matter to the work.

The term "structured interviewing" refers both to the process of enhancing the standardization and job relatedness of the interview.

Extensive research has focused on how to structure the interview, and many helpful approaches and techniques have been identified. These techniques are relatively easy to use for the benefits they deliver. Examples include ways of enhancing the content of the interview, like basing questions on a careful analysis of the job requirements and asking the same or similar questions across candidates, and enhancing the process of evaluating candidate answers, like using rating scales and taking notes.

The goal of this book is to explain some of the most important ways to structure an interview. In my opinion, the book has done an excellent job of this. And it is written in an easily accessible and practical way that makes the material interesting and intuitive, while still being educational and technically sophisticated.

– Michael A. Campion

PREFACE

Science matters!

After decades of research, we can clearly and definitively state that what makes one an accomplished interviewer does not lie in some innate ability to peer into the depths of someone's character or an uncanny knack for asking the "right" question that reveals everything the interviewer needs to know. Rather, the techniques and practices that contribute to accurate, successful interviews are well documented in the scientific literature and can be taught and transferred to just about anyone who is motivated to learn them.

If that is the case, then why would anyone not apply the available science to a process as important as interviewing and selecting talent for the organization? There are a number of possibilities.

They may not agree with the importance of the process. Unfortunate. Most leaders in business today agree that it's the people who make the difference and that the competitor with the best talent will win. Furthermore, the results of multiple human capital ROI studies strongly support this position. Getting the best people and making the best people decisions is as close to a no-brainer as you are going to get.

They may not like doing it the right way. Also unfortunate. Doing interviews the right way does change the way most people interview. It does require interviewers to do specific things a certain way. So, most people will have to change the way they interview in order to make better decisions.

They may find it too hard to do. You guessed it, unfortunate as well.

Shifting frames of reference then, it may be that they are not aware of the science. Good point, but there probably isn't an HR professional on the planet who isn't at least generally aware of the 100 years of research behind more accurate and better interviewing. So, the science is on board and close at hand.

They may not agree with the science. Fair, but who would ever argue that not planning for an interview is better than planning? Who would argue that inconsistency outperforms consistency? Who would argue that applying more accurate criteria and rigor to the interview process would not increase accuracy?

Finally, they may agree with the science, but not know with confidence how to apply it the right way. Very fair. Understanding and mastering the right way to interview based on what the scientific research has taught us is what this book is really about.

What's interesting about the particular application of science to interviewing is that people readily apply many of the same analyses and decision-making techniques described here to other areas of life. The informal, casual interviewing common to most organizations is done without much planning or foresight. Aside from scanning the resume and having some idea of what you might be looking for, there is not much preparation. It is primarily a free-flowing, off-the-cuff conversation with a few stock questions thrown in here and there. There is also not much rigor or consistency in how interview responses are evaluated.

In contrast, we are generally quite focused and thorough in other areas of life that involve making critical decisions. Consider the process of buying a house. You and your family begin by creating a set of characteristics you are looking for. Good schools. Big kitchen. A fenced yard for the dog. Lots of light. A playroom for the kids. Close enough to work. You give the requirements to an agent who screens properties for you, or you may even do that yourself using the Internet. When you visit properties, you check off your absolutes and your nice-to-haves. When you have looked at multiple properties, you put your findings on a spreadsheet (on paper or in your mind) and compare the properties against the criteria. The fundamentals are all there: thoughtful preparation, deliberate data gathering, and careful analysis. The same might apply to a car purchase, a school choice, or a new computer.

From a selection standpoint, the same findings apply to a professional sports draft. Teams ask themselves, What do we need? What characteristics are we looking for? Next, they look at the available candidates in a consistent or rigorous way (with scouting reports, references from coaches, and tryout camps). Then they compare possible draft choices side by side on a spreadsheet and pick the best one that is available when their choice comes up.

So, the general findings of the research we will be discussing—knowing what you are looking for ahead of time, applying those criteria in a consistent way, and objectively evaluating multiple candidates on the equivalent of a spreadsheet—are things we all do willingly in other areas of our lives.

Following the prescriptions laid out in this book will improve everyone's "hit rate," or success, as an interviewer. You will make better people decisions by being prepared and applying rigor to the process.

And yes, it's probably going to be different from how you do it now.

Sorry, that's the price of success.

INTRODUCTION

Ken Taylor checked his watch. It was 9:52. His morning staff meeting, due to end at 9:30, had run longer than expected. At least he had a few moments to prep for his 10:00 interview with Amy Thompson, a candidate for HomeCo's Director of Advertising. As he rose through the ranks at HomeCo to become Vice President of Sales & Marketing, Ken had learned to value the open spaces in his increasingly crowded schedule of meetings and conference calls.

Ken cleared some space at his conference table and hit the Do Not Disturb button on his phone. A quick check of his voice mail told him that Amy had already arrived in the lobby. Ken knew that time was of the essence. He only had until 11:00 to meet with Amy, and then he was scheduled to talk with HomeCo's CFO about some difficulties with processing rebates from a recent sales promotion. In keeping with his precise management of HomeCo's finances, the CFO did not appreciate late starts.

As he was leaving the office the day before, Ken received an e-mail from one of HomeCo's senior recruiters with Amy's resume attached. He had printed it out and glanced over it in his home office that evening. Now he picked it up again and tried to refresh his memory.

As Ken looked over Amy's background and accomplishments, he quickly remembered why she had come to him with high praise from the recruiting staff and other members of his team who had spoken with her previously. On paper, at least, she seemed to have it all—an MBA from a Top 30 program, experience working across multiple advertising channels, and a five-year stint at a respected ad agency. Most intriguing of all, she had done creative work on the advertising account for one of HomeCo's primary retail customers, Dzine Emporium. Hopefully, her past experience and relationships would be integral in helping to launch joint advertising campaigns and further HomeCo's efforts at co-branding.

Ken had seen quite a few "final" candidates for this position over the previous four months and hoped this would be the end of the search. The previous candidates all had suitable credentials but none had worked out. One candidate was a young rising star in product design at a HomeCo competitor but had little real-world experience in marketing and advertising. Promising, but not worth the gamble, Ken felt. Another seemed to be full of great creative ideas but was so lacking in social skills that Ken was worried what might happen if he took him to lunch meetings with customers. An offer had been extended to one candidate, a solid performer at a large beverage company, who turned down HomeCo when her employer countered with a promotion. Ken hated losing, so naturally the incident had gotten under his skin. He wondered what Amy's expectations might be and if HomeCo could meet them.

Adding to his concern, he knew how critical the advertising role was to HomeCo's growth plans. HomeCo had been in the consumer goods marketplace for over 50 years and created some durable flagship products. Yet they were still somewhat unknown to the average consumer and had not established a clear corporate identity. Space had been created in the annual budget for a national campaign to draw attention to the breadth of HomeCo's product offerings; now they just needed the right person to launch it.

As Ken left his office and strode down to the sunlit lobby to meet with Amy, he thought back to his own stint as Director of Advertising. In fact, his success in that assignment had put him on the track to become a vice president. Since becoming VP six years ago, he had hired two other people into the advertising role, but neither of them seemed to sustain much of a spark and eventually found their way to other opportunities outside HomeCo. Such had been the case with some of Ken's other direct reports, and now he felt he had no clear successor in place. Ken needed to find someone who was not only a "keeper" for the advertising role, but also had the potential and drive to continue up the ladder.

"Hi, you must be Amy. Ken Taylor."

"Nice to meet you, Ken," replied Amy. "Diane at Dzine says hello." Then she added with a sly grin, "She said to remind you that you still haven't made good on that bet you lost on the golf course last year."

Ken chuckled, shook his head and said, "She never lets go, does she?"

"No, she sure doesn't," Amy laughed back.

The reference to losing out on the bet to Diane caused Ken to wince inside for just a second. But at the same time he thought to himself that a sharp sense of humor never held anyone back at HomeCo; you needed to be able to give and take a little bit. He also thought it was a good sign that she was staying in touch with the folks at Dzine and probably doing some due diligence on HomeCo.

As they headed down the plush main hallway, lined on either side with HomeCo's latest products, they engaged in some small talk about Amy's prior interviews at HomeCo. As they talked, Ken found himself impressed with Amy's poise and professionalism. She had a confident, yet even-keeled, presence that conveyed a willingness to take charge but not overpower others. Ken thought how that might balance against his blunt, sometimes off-putting style.

"Go ahead and have a seat," Ken said as they reached the door of his corner office overlooking the landscaped grounds of HomeCo's headquarters. "I'm going to grab some water. Care for any?"

"Sure, that would be great," replied Amy as she took a look at the various plaques and awards that dotted the shelves of Ken's office.

The trip to fetch water was intentional on Ken's part. Despite his swagger and confidence in dealing with others, he always felt a bit of apprehension when it came to conducting interviews. Sometimes he felt that the demands of trying to sell the company and create a rapport with a future direct report got in the way of trying to assess whether or not the person might be a good fit for his team and for HomeCo. Plus, there was always the pressure of picking the right person. Sure, he had some successful hires to talk about, but no genuine superstars. Besides that, he'd also hired his share of flameouts. This always seemed a bit odd to Ken, since his initial background in sales had taught him to read others and make judgments about someone's character.

After returning with the water and taking a seat at the conference table, Ken wasted no time in filling Amy in on his vision for the advertising function and for sales and marketing overall. In doing so, he recounted some of his own experiences in advertising. He was pleased to hear that Amy was familiar with some of his work on earlier campaigns and had even purchased a fair number of HomeCo's products.

After a while, Ken said, "Well, enough about what I've done. I'd like to hear more about some of your experiences."

"Sure thing," said Amy. "What can I tell you?"

Ken retrieved her resume from his portfolio and gave it a glance. He immediately focused in on her experience working as Assistant Creative Director on the Dzine Emporium account during her ad agency days. It had been four years ago, but he wanted to see what she had accomplished in that role. As Amy told her story from that experience, Ken reflected back on the particular print and TV advertisements she described and recalled that it wasn't some of the strongest work he had seen. Too splashy, he thought, not enough substance. Still, he liked hearing her insights about Dzine's culture and enjoyed sharing tales about some people they knew in common. Besides, Ken reflected, she wasn't in the position of making final decisions on the account, so she couldn't be held completely accountable for what was produced.

As he talked with Amy about some of her other roles and accomplishments, Ken would occasionally jot some remarks on her resume to indicate things such as a particularly noteworthy achievement or a questionable turn in her career path. They had begun to discuss Amy's most recent role as Marketing Manager for a small, but emerging, software firm when Amy's attention was drawn to a photograph of Ken's family during a recent trip to Rome.

"Oh, I see you've been to Italy!" exclaimed Amy.

"Yes," said Ken, caught a bit off guard, "we took a trip to Rome last June. We stopped there for three days before heading off to Athens for a week."

Amy then spent the next several minutes describing how she spent a semester abroad in Milan during college and stayed the summer to intern at one of the trendier fashion companies. Ken found her description of her experience as further evidence of her well-roundedness as well as her grasp of consumer culture. However, he didn't feel that he could relate particularly well to her stories about the plazas and cathedrals of Milan since he had never visited there. Ken listened with what he felt was appropriate interest, but he was also a little irked because he knew that the clock was ticking down to his 11:00 meeting.

Ken checked his watch again to see that it was now 10:48. He wanted to take a moment to respond to any particular questions Amy might have, but first he felt compelled to ask a few of his mainstay questions: "Tell me about the key qualities you look for in a job," and "Tell me when you realized that you wanted to be in advertising." Amy's response to the first question was pretty well in line with what Ken had heard from previous candidates: opportunities to tackle unique challenges, to be creative, and to create a well-respected portfolio of work. The answer to the second question intrigued him. Amy didn't cite, as others had, a favorite TV commercial or a fascination with media. Instead, she spoke about a course she took in consumer psychology that gave her a different understanding of how messages are created in the media that have a subtle, yet powerful, influence on consumers' perceptions and buying habits. Previously, Amy had been on a path to become a clinical or counseling psychologist, but then saw the opportunity to merge her interest in psychology with the world of business and commerce.

Unfortunately, Ken thought, he would have to reflect more on the decision later. It was time to see Amy off and then scramble to his meeting with the CFO. As they walked back down the hall, Ken fielded a few questions from Amy about HomeCo's recent quarterly performance and whether they would be expanding their e-commerce ventures.

In the lobby, Ken reached out his hand to shake Amy's and said, "It was great meeting you. We'll get back in touch with you soon; a week at the most, I hope."

"That would be great," replied Amy. "I'm really excited about this opportunity. Thanks again for your time, Ken."

Ken stood for a moment as she exited the glass doors to the front parking lot, then he quickly headed back down the hall.

****

Later in the day, after a long, tense meeting with the CFO and a lunch appointment with an important retail buyer, Ken was walking back to his office when he heard the phone on his desk ringing. He dashed inside, set down his briefcase, and picked up the phone. It was Carl Benson, the senior recruiter who first contacted Amy. "So," said Carl, in his booming voice, "how did it go with Amy?" Ken paused and said, "Well, let me think...."

CHAPTER 1

THE SCIENTIFIC AND PRACTICAL CASE FOR PREPARATION, CONSISTENCY, AND RIGOR

While many interviewers will attest to their strong ability to read others and be a good judge of character in an interview, their intuition in these areas does not necessarily serve them well when it comes to making hiring decisions. In fact, research has shown that the probability of making a successful hiring decision when following a typical set of informal, casual interview practices is roughly equivalent to making the decision by flipping a coin (Hunter & Hunter, 1984). Unfortunately, the gambler's fallacy can set in, and as successful hires add up, it becomes easier to overlook the losses.

What does it mean to follow a more rigorous and science-based interviewing process? Basically, it involves three things. First, pre-interview planning involves knowing what you are looking for ahead of time. What are the critical skills, competencies, and perspectives needed for successful performance? What elements of background and experience tend to predict those skills? Next, conducting the interview involves asking specific preplanned questions and looking for specific answers or themes. It also involves asking the same questions of multiple candidates for the same job. It means less talking and more listening. It also means taking relevant notes. Finally, post-interview evaluation involves using data-based rigor in comparing candidates. Referencing vague impressions and day-old memories won't do. So, structured interviewing is a three-stage process: preplanning, conducting the interview properly, and applying rigor in the evaluation that follows.

Returning to the story of Ken and Amy's interview, you may have thought to yourself that nothing in particular seemed out of place. There appeared to be an even, back-and-forth exchange and an opportunity to share stories and perspectives. Amy had the opportunity to demonstrate her accomplishments as well as get a feel for what Ken might expect from her. While she may have made a misstep here and there, she certainly didn't do anything to embarrass herself or raise any red flags.

As you neared the end of the story, you may also have felt a sense of uncertainty starting to set in. Would Ken recommend Amy for hire? If so, how strong would the recommendation be? Would she be someone who could grow in the role, or would it be another year or so before Ken found himself back in the same place, sitting down with another candidate?

Put yourself in Ken's shoes for a moment. How easy would it be to provide a solid conclusion as to whether or not Amy would be the right person for the role? He might have a gut feeling pushing him in one direction or the other, but beyond that, what has he really learned from the interview? Does he have the information he needs to predict if Amy can demonstrate the behaviors critical for long-term success at the director level and beyond? She's had some interesting experiences that could be very valuable in her role at HomeCo, but how much has she really learned from them? Can she apply those lessons to a new and different set of experiences?

The reason Ken might find himself standing at the crossroads of uncertainty has nothing to do with anything "wrong" he did in the interview. If anything, he followed an approach that is typical. The job interview has become an institutionalized practice in selecting new employees and, like most typical practices, very little has changed over the years. As a result, many managers, including experienced interviewers like Ken, are left to trust a few noteworthy observations plus their instincts when it comes to making critical decisions about whom to hire and not hire.

The costs associated with making a poor or even suboptimal hiring decision are many and great. The financial costs are the most obvious. A study found that the costs associated with making a failed hire at the upper-managerial level can be as much as three times that person's base salary plus benefits (Corporate Leadership Council, 1998). That's $300,000 for a $100,000 manager.

And that's just accounting for matters such as salary, benefits, severance pay, headhunting fees, and training costs. It doesn't begin to factor in the likelihood of lost productivity, slumping revenues, declines in customer satisfaction, and turnover costs. Don't forget the lurking danger of expensive and drawn-out legal proceedings that can crop up because of things that shouldn't have been said or done during the interview itself. If that weren't enough, lost opportunity costs as a result of not hiring the right person also need to be considered. Meanwhile, your competitors may be gaining on you in the war for talent if they are better at interviewing than you are.

In light of the sobering statistics mentioned above, there's good news to offer about interviewing—very good news. Over the past several decades, a steady mountain of research and real-world results has built up in support of taking a planned and rigorous approach to the interview and focusing attention on specific behaviors critical to performance. It's generally called the structured interview. Side-by-side comparisons of structured, behavior-based interviewing with an informal, casual, and unstructured interviewing process show that the structured approach is consistently more accurate, oftentimes by more than a 2 to 1 ratio (Conway, Jako, & Goodman, 1995; Huffcutt & Arthur, 1994; McDaniel, Whetzel, Schmidt, & Maurer, 1994; Schmidt & Hunter, 1998; Wiesner & Cronshaw, 1988; Wright, Lichtenfels, & Pursell, 1989).

So, if there is such clear and convincing evidence that planning and rigor—or structured interviewing—is a superior approach, why don't more organizations and managers engage in the practice? It's a bit like the old tale with diet and exercise. We've all heard since we were children that certain practices will lead to a longer and healthier life, but the vast majority of us tend to do our own thing until we get to a certain stage in life and then decide to try something different. Often we need a compelling reason to make such a change. The call to action can be either positive or negative. The same goes for interviewing. You might be dismayed at the disappointing performance of an employee that everyone thought was a sure thing based on his or her career trajectory and track record of accomplishments. On the flip side, the realization that you spend a significant amount of your waking hours at work or that you want to leave behind a talent legacy you can be proud of may motivate you to learn how to hire more productive and longer-lasting employees. Whatever your reason, find it, and you'll be on the path to more accurate interviewing and hiring.

Misconceptions and/or fear of the unknown also discourage people from adopting healthier habits. "Exercise is boring. I'm a free spirit—I don't like being on a regimen. Is it too late to even make a difference? I know someone who

Why Berbee Switched to Structured Interviewing

Our compelling reason to implement a better interviewing method was cost-driven. As the organization's pace for growth began to accelerate in 2002, it became increasingly important to make good hiring choices. The more hiring you do, the more mistakes you can make, and thus, the more you increase costs, lose productivity, and even affect morale. In the year prior to implementing our structured, competency-based interviewing and selection process, we calculated that our hiring mistakes amounted to over half a million dollars. Because our ROI calculation was based on conservative data, the actual cost was likely higher. Either way, the financial impact of our hiring decisions led us to realize that we needed to implement a more rigorous and effective approach.

– Marilyn Westmas

3

ate fast food every day and lived to be 90." The list goes on and on. With more structured interviewing, some managers may feel like they are being taken out of their preferred style or method of interviewing. "My interviewing track record has always been fine. Why can't I do it my way anymore?" they might say. Others might feel confined by the structured approach. "I enjoy the back-and-forth of a good conversation. Plus, I'm more of a talker, not a listener." Still others might be concerned about the impression left on the candidate. "Won't they get bored? Will their impressions of the organization be negative?" The research done to date hasn't provided any substantive evidence for these claims, nor do the feedback comments from interviewers and candidates, when the structured interview process follows best practices (Campion, Palmer, & Campion, 1997).

Once you've invested some time in learning and practicing the more structured approach, the benefits will start to emerge, and you will also find that it can be a very engaging and even fun activity. Just like those individuals who get hooked on a healthier lifestyle, you may find yourself wondering at some point why you didn't do it this way all along.

Before we start taking you through all the benefits and how-to's associated with using a structured behavioral approach to interviewing, a few more words are in order about how interviews are typically conducted in organizations and some of the subtle and not-so-subtle shortcomings that can emerge.

Typical Interview Practices. Most Common Mistakes.

There is no record of the first-ever job interview, but our guess is that it took place a long, long time ago. Perhaps Ogg was looking for an additional hunter for his woolly mammoth team. Except for the fact that the conversation wasn't interrupted by beeping pagers and cell phones, it was probably much like one you would experience today. So what are some of the more common elements of the job interview?

- **It doesn't last very long.** A study reported that the average interview lasts just under 40 minutes. Even more interesting, the standard deviation (plus or minus variation) was 25 minutes. This means that only a small percentage of interviews are longer than an hour, and it would not necessarily be out of the ordinary for an interview to last only about 15 minutes (Campion, Palmer, & Campion, 1997).

- **Roughly equal attention is given to delivering and gathering information.** In most organizations, interviews have a dual function: part opportunity to size up potential employees and part opportunity to sell the candidate on the organization.

- **The tone is often informal and unstructured.** A good part of the interview is often focused on building rapport and developing a good "feel" for the candidate. In the course of doing so, the conversation can often flow from topic to topic, depending on the interests of either party.

- **The content from interview to interview is inconsistent.** Interviewers often resort to a small subset of standard questions that they may use with any candidate. Other than that, the content is more likely to vary, depending on the candidate's background and what topics come up during the conversation. Even interviews with candidates for the same position often do not overlap very much in terms of content. This makes comparing candidates difficult.

- **Note taking is limited.** Some interviewers are copious note takers by nature, but the majority like to record a few particular observations or underline noteworthy information here and there on the resume. Long stretches can go by during the interview where no note taking occurs at all.

- **The primary focus is on technical abilities and individual achievements.** Once they have an intuitive sense of whether or not they can work with a person, interviewers often shift their attention to determining if the individual has the requisite skills and abilities to perform the job on a day-to-day basis. Thus, more attention is focused on aspects of the candidate's knowledge base and track record of accomplishments than on factors such as strategic thinking skills, getting work done through others, or handling difficult situations with courage and composure.

- **The resume often dictates the content of the interview.** A well-written resume is a great marketing tool. It not only gets a candidate noticed, but it can also influence what others choose to ask questions about. Consequently, if it's a question that pertains to something on the candidate's resume, he or she will likely have prepared a quick response that portrays the achievement in the most positive light (Andler, 1998).

- **Traditional questions are frequently met with canned and rehearsed responses.** Beyond the resume-specific questions that candidates can often easily respond to, there are also the time-honored favorites of the corporate interview, the most infamous being "Tell me your greatest strengths and weaknesses." These questions and the responses that follow often provoke an "I've heard that before" reaction from both the candidate and the interviewer.

5

- **Criteria for evaluating a candidate are often narrow or unclear.** Sometimes interviewers sit down with a candidate in an effort to gauge the individual's "fit," but have difficulty defining what does or does not represent that fit. In other instances, a specific set of criteria is laid out, but why those particular factors have been chosen or if they capture a complete set of behaviors critical for performance is unclear.

Again, these practices are not necessarily always bad. Many managers simply find them the easiest and most acceptable things to do, given the perceived constraints of the interview format as well as the confines of their busy schedules. However, these typical practices often pave the way for some common interviewing mistakes. While not every problem listed below finds its way into each and every interview situation, at least a couple of them tend to appear in any interview.

- **Lack of preparation.** Sometimes the opportunity to conduct a successful interview is in jeopardy before the conversation even begins. Without a clear understanding of the role and the competencies needed to tackle it successfully, and how key behaviors can be spotted in the interview, the rest of the effort will lack focus and effectiveness. Nevertheless, whether because of limited time or a belief in their ability to read others, many interviewers wind up "winging it" when it comes time to conduct the interview.

- **Overweighing first impressions.** One of the most cited interview studies came to the conclusion that most interviewers reach a near-firm decision on hiring within the first three minutes of meeting a candidate (Springbett, 1958). In these cases, the remainder of the interview exists to either search for more information that confirms initial positive impressions or go through the motions until the session can be called to an end. As a result, important information is often overlooked or doesn't have the opportunity to surface in the discussion.

- **Insufficient data gathering.** As we mentioned earlier, note taking is often limited and sporadic. Consequently, the interviewer misses the opportunity to record impressions in real time. This limits the amount of clear information to draw from when discussing the candidate with others and trying to reach final conclusions later.

- **Making too much of a negative.** At least three to four pieces of positive information are needed to balance out a negative impression recorded during the interview (Miller & Rowe, 1967). Some interviewers' tendencies to want to "screen out" candidates by looking for a so-called red flag or knock-out punch make it difficult to make objective evaluations.

- **Fix-it-later assumptions.** Individuals who adhere to fix-it-later assumptions are often so taken with a candidate's numerous positive qualities that they are willing to overlook issues that could potentially result in serious problems down the road. A frequent example is when a candidate with superior technical skills is extended an offer despite clear evidence of low interpersonal skills. The interviewer assumes that the candidate's interpersonal shortcomings can be addressed over time while he or she continues to make a positive impact in the technical arena. Sometimes this story has a happy ending, but the more frequent result is a call to HR or an expensive executive coach.

- **Overemphasizing fit.** Research suggests that person-organization or person-culture fit is an important element in retention and long-term success on the job (Schneider, 1987). However, it is not the only factor of relevance and should be appropriately balanced with other considerations in making the hiring decision.

- **Focusing on irrelevant behaviors.** Sometimes the interviewer's attention is drawn to a behavior that is intriguing yet has little relevance to performance on the job. A candidate might make an impression with her interpersonal savvy and poise in dealing with others. However, if the role she is a candidate for is mostly behind the scenes and offers little opportunity to entertain or influence others, how valuable are those skills?

- **Biased/leading questions.** Even the most experienced interviewers will occasionally provide too much information to lead the candidate. Asking closed-ended questions that result in the candidate giving factual or yes/no answers is also an easy trap to fall into. The candidate might appreciate the ease of responding to these types of questions, but they provide little in the way of valuable information for the interviewer.

- **Hasty evaluation and decision making.** Thorough preparation and an expertly conducted interview can be quickly undone by poor handling of the decision-making process. Hiring panels can begin to let personal biases and agendas influence the final outcome when faced with limited information and time pressure.

Following a structured, behavior-based approach to interviewing minimizes or eliminates many of these mistakes. The remaining chapters explain why and how this happens.

Does Person-Organization Fit Really Matter?

Both experienced and inexperienced interviewers often believe that the fit between the person and the organization is a critical factor in determining the outcome of a hiring decision. It turns out that the amount of statistical variability in hiring decisions that is accounted for by actual measured similarity between the values of the candidate and the values of the organization is quite small.

In a typical study on this topic, the cultural values of the organization and the individual candidates are measured using independent surveys. The cultural values include such things as the importance of autonomy on the job, being team oriented, employment security, risk taking, rule oriented, results oriented, emphasis on quality, and many others. The actual similarity is calculated by computer and not known to the interviewer. Later this measure of similarity is correlated with the interviewer's hiring decisions. The results show that only about 1% or 2% of the variation in hiring decisions is explained by actual similarity in cultural values.

There are many possible reasons for this outcome. Possibly the candidates' credentials are more important than cultural values. Or possibly candidates that appear to "fit" one organization, fit many organizations. In other words, good candidates fit lots of organizations. Whatever the explanation, the suggestion from this research is not to make too much out of presumed culture fit in your hiring decisions.

– Michael A. Campion

Example study: Cable, D.M., & Judge, T.A. (1997).

Nobody Said It Was Easy

Interviewing and making accurate decisions is not an inherently simple or easy process. A variety of challenges facing the interviewer makes it easier for mistakes to occur. Some are obvious; others tend to lurk in the background. Here are five critical challenges interviewers face:

(1) **Time pressure:** Time pressure exists on two levels: micro and macro. On the smaller scale, a limited amount of time often exists to gather meaningful information from a candidate—interview sessions are seldom scheduled for more than an hour. On the larger scale, recruiters and managers experience pressure to fill open positions in a timely manner. Having a position stay open longer than expected only raises the pressure.

8

(2) **Decision pressure:** Making a hiring decision is never a trivial task, but the pressure on making a good call tends to increase with the level and salary of the position.

(3) **Ambiguity:** This challenge is a given. No matter what your experience as an interviewer or the amount of time taken, you will never learn everything you need or want to know about a candidate. Interviewers need to be able to deal comfortably and effectively with loose ends. Unfortunately, many individuals find doing so very difficult.

(4) **Social expectations:** Both candidates and interviewers tend to be on their best behavior. Neither party wants to look bad to the other. While commendable, this mind-set can also lead to acting out of character and telling the other party what we think they want to hear. As a result, a positively distorted image can form on both sides and both parties will ultimately pay the price.

(5) **Process and logistics:** Sometimes the coordination, complexity, and level of secrecy that accompany scheduling an interview for an executive-level candidate can rival that of a major military campaign. Oftentimes these steps are necessary, but they also sap time, energy, and focus away from the real task—determining if the person is right for the role. Similar challenges can occur in assigning responsibilities to an interview panel and then getting panel members to share their observations and make a decision. As a result, standardization of interview practices is often an afterthought.

Some of these challenges, such as ambiguity, will never be completely eliminated, but a best practices approach to interviewing makes many of them more manageable.

The Advantages of Structured Interviewing

Following the interviewing approach we describe in this book is not just about eliminating mistakes or making the process more manageable; substantial benefits can also be gained. Here are just a few:

- **Improved hiring:** Structured, behavior-based interviewing is one of the most valid forms of selection. Structured interviews also demonstrate lower levels of adverse impact (see box below) than cognitive abilities tests, another popular selection tool (Huffcutt & Roth, 1998). Furthermore, applicant reactions to interviews are more favorable when compared to other selection methods such as personality tests, biodata inventories, integrity tests, and some forms of cognitive abilities tests (Moscoso & Salgado, 2004; Smither, Reilly, Millsap, Pearlman, & Stoffey, 1993).

- **Clarity and comfort:** When you conduct a structured interview that focuses on abilities mission critical to job performance, you know what you are looking for and how to determine if a candidate possesses those abilities. The ambiguity and uncertainty experienced by the interviewer decreases and confidence increases. Consequently, there is less likelihood of "missing something" in the interview.

- **Standardization:** A structured, consistent interview process creates an even playing field for evaluating candidates for a position. Interviewers share a common language and a common yardstick for comparing candidates' strengths and weaknesses.

- **Easier maintenance:** Clearly defined roles for interviewers. Established criteria for evaluating candidates. Specified links between job requirements and interview content. All of these elements make it easier to train individuals how to interview and evaluate the ongoing effectiveness of the organization's interviewing practices.

What Is Adverse Impact?

"Adverse impact" is a technical term with important legal implications. Adverse impact is determined by comparing the hiring rates of minority group candidates to non-minority group candidates, or women candidates to men candidates. For example, if you hired 45% of women candidates and 50% of men candidates, then the impact on women would be 45% divided by 50%, or .90. If the impact is below .80, then adverse impact is said to occur. If it is above .80, then adverse impact has not occurred. In other words, adverse impact is when the hiring rate of one group is less than 80% or 4/5ths the hiring rate of the other group.

Adverse impact is important because federal hiring regulations stipulate that when adverse impact occurs, the organization is required to prove that its hiring procedure is job related; otherwise, it is illegal. Many companies have been sued for adverse impact and lost millions of dollars in damages and attorneys' fees.

Structured interviews tend to show less adverse impact compared with other good hiring procedures such as employment aptitude tests. Tests can sometimes show adverse impact against some minority groups, although not usually against women.

– Michael A. Campion

Reference: Equal Employment Opportunity Commission, Civil Service Commission, Department of Labor, & Department of Justice (1978).

> ### The Value of a Repeatable Process
>
> In the high-tech industry, we've learned that we can reduce time, eliminate errors, and increase the quality of the result if we operate in a repeatable process framework. With a repeatable process, there is a planned route and specific, proven tools to use. For us at Berbee, the Lominger model is our repeatable interview process. Each interview set is customized for the position requirements, but the routine and methods are always the same. The interview team and the hiring manager know what to expect and get very good at their part. We have quickly become more efficient and more skilled in our questioning and evaluation techniques.
>
> *– Marilyn Westmas*

- **Strengthened defensibility:** The prospect of litigation always hovers over selection decisions. Legal research shows that structured interviews stand up very well in court (Williamson, Campion, Malos, Roehling, & Campion, 1997).

- **Selection-development alignment:** Think of the observations gathered from the interview as a first snapshot of a new employee entering the organization. Evaluating behaviors critical to job performance gives you an immediate assessment of where an employee stands. Developmental needs identified during the interview can be addressed immediately via specially designed job assignments.

The key to achieving these advantages lies in mastering three critical steps in the interview process.

Just three steps? Tell me more.

Stage is a more appropriate term than step. A lot of attention tends to get focused on the interview itself. The pre- and post-interview stages do not always get the same scrutiny. However, critical mistakes can happen at any stage and each is essential to a successful interview. Preparing for, conducting, and evaluating the interview make up the proverbial three-legged stool of interviewing practices. Chapters 2 through 4 focus on each individual stage and provide a variety of how-to steps and practical tips.

11

Following the essentials, the final three chapters help you take interviewing to the next level. Chapter 5 outlines some skills for more advanced interviewers to master. Chapter 6 tackles emerging trends and unanswered questions related to interviewing. Chapter 7 identifies the critical skills an interviewer needs to be effective and offers tips for development.

Interviewing is always full of surprises and insights. It's something you can become very good at, but no matter how many interviews you've conducted, there is always something new to learn. This book will provide you with lessons to build a good foundation. Embrace your experiences as an interviewer, and they will be a source of continued growth and enrichment as well as a competitive advantage.

Court Cases on Employment Interviews

Structured interviews have been shown to be more legally defensible in court than traditional interviews. A study of 99 federal court cases on employment interviews identified the characteristics of interviews statistically associated with judgments in favor of the organization (defendant). These characteristics are the unmistakable features of structured interviews.

They were:
- Objective/job-related criteria
- Behavior (versus trait) based criteria
- Specific (versus general) criteria
- Trained interviewer
- Interviewer familiar with job requirements
- Validation (job relatedness) evidence
- Guidelines for conducting interview
- Minimal interviewer discretion
- Standardized questions
- Consistent administration
- Interviewer's decision reviewed

– Michael A. Campion
Reference: Williamson, L.G., Campion, J.E., Malos, S.B., Roehling, M.V., & Campion, M.A. (1997).

CHAPTER 2

PREPARING FOR A COMPETENCY INTERVIEW

Preparation sets the tone. Preparation leads to clarity and focus in the interview. If you don't prepare, sooner or later, no matter what your experience, you will make inaccurate judgments. Interviewers who are unprepared tend to experience more difficulty with asking consistent questions and clearly evaluating candidates' answers (Rosenberg, 2000).

So how hard could it be to get ready for the interview? Some challenges and pitfalls common to this stage require some careful thought and decision making.

The first consideration is determining the purpose of the interview. Before you can determine *what* you are looking for, let alone *how* you will look for it, you need to decide *why* you are meeting the candidate in the first place. What do you hope to gain from sitting down with this individual? What decisions or next steps will follow the interview?

Recruiting? Assessment? A Little of Both?

Interviews can serve many purposes. Interviews can promote the image of an organization, serve to attract top talent, assess culture fit, or evaluate a candidate's skill set. Decisions need to be made regarding what types of interviews the candidate will go through, when they will occur in the hiring process, and who will conduct them.

The important thing to recognize now is that the type of interview will influence the content and structure of the conversation. When the interviewer has not made a clear decision beforehand about interview type, the process often floats back and forth between efforts at recruiting and assessment. Neither party tends to walk away from the interview learning much of what they hoped.

The best results occur when the interview addresses a single, well-defined purpose. That isn't to say that a recruiting interview can't feature a probing question or two. A few minutes at the beginning and end of an assessment interview for small talk and candidate questions isn't out of place either. At the very least, an 80-20 rule should apply.

Generally speaking, there are six types of interviews that might be applied, depending upon the nature of the open position:

The first type is the **general screening interview**. The primary focus here is doing a rough "in or out" screen. The candidate should receive information about the position and the organization. This includes getting a realistic job preview that details some of the pros and cons that should be expected. This sets a tone of fair play and open exchange. It also allows candidates to self-select out of a situation that doesn't fit their needs and interests. The candidate should be given ample opportunity to ask questions. At this stage, the interviewer (usually a member of recruiting or HR) should review the candidate's work history for minimal qualifications in terms of experience and credentials.

The second type is the **functional/technical skills evaluation.** This should be administered by someone who has a high level of technical expertise in the area in question. The objective is to make sure the candidate has sufficient "hard" skills—engineering, computer science, chemistry, finance, etc.—to perform daily job tasks as expected.

The third type is the **culture fit assessment**. The focus here is whether the candidate—regardless of other qualifications—would fit well in the culture surrounding the job. Would others already there accept and work well with this person? This type of interview is best done by an HR professional intimately familiar with all aspects of the organization's culture.

The fourth type is the **competency interview**. The focus here is whether the candidate has the specific skills and competencies (in addition to functional/technical skills) required to be able to perform well in the job. Several individuals may participate in this stage, including the hiring manager and peers.

The fifth type is the **learning agility interview**. The focus here is whether, once in place at the enterprise, the candidate will be able to continue to learn and grow into jobs of greater scope and responsibility. The concept is to assess whether the candidate has the potential of a full career after joining the company. This should be conducted by someone with special training in this area, often a member of recruiting or HR.

The sixth type is the **sales interview**, or the close. This should either be the direct boss and/or the HR person. The task is to sell the person on the job and the organization. In this type of interview, the interviewer does most of the talking. It's a sales interview.

This book focuses on competency interviews.

What Is a Competency?

A competency is a measurable characteristic related to work success. Most competencies are behavioral in nature and can be observed. A few are grounded in the knowledge gained from our experiences. Competencies cover a broad range of performance characteristics, from Strategic Agility to Process Management to Compassion.

Competencies are broad and universal. Competencies are not limited to a particular job type or organizational level. Jobs as diverse as controller and customer service representative share competencies such as Conflict Management, Problem Solving, and Integrity and Trust. All the competencies that have been defined to date account for 50% to 60% of the behaviors related to success at work (Lombardo & Eichinger, 2004).

Competencies are somewhat distinct from one another. Competencies such as Action Oriented and Drive for Results may appear similar on the surface but have unique behavioral definitions. Individuals strong in one may not be in the other.

Competencies also have different developmental paths—they may be learned differently. Some are more difficult to master than others, and different experiences play a role in learning and skill building. While an individual who is not Action Oriented and another who is low in Drive for Results may both experience difficulty with addressing the bottom line, they will require different types of coaching and developmental challenges to strengthen their performance.

Competencies have a defined structure. Many competency libraries exist. They have different names for many competencies, and definitions vary in complexity, but they cover much of the same ground. They also share similar underlying structures. The good news here is that you don't need to define a set of competencies from scratch. Just make sure the model you choose is supported by research and is adaptable to your needs.

Competencies are versatile. Competencies have many applications beyond their use in selection and interviewing. Competencies play an important role in areas such as leadership development, performance management, and succession planning. Using the same set of competencies for different purposes better aligns and integrates your organization's people practices.

Competencies matter. Competency development has been tied to a variety of outcomes critical to organizational success, including reduced turnover, increased sales, rises in productivity, and stronger profits (Lombardo & Eichinger, 2004). The results are real and impressive. By selecting for the competencies critical to long-term performance, you can add to your organization's talent pool for success.

An Example – Lominger's Competency Library

Lominger's library was assembled over 15 years ago and originates from research first conducted by the authors at the Center for Creative Leadership (Lombardo & Eichinger, 1989). Since the library was introduced in the early 1990s, competency data has been collected from thousands of employees in over 140 organizations. The library database is regularly updated, and a fresh study is conducted every two years.

Consistent results have emerged from the research. Our library contains 67 distinct competencies. The 67 competencies are organized into a framework of six factors or categories. The factors break down into a set of 21 clusters of two or more competencies. The library is depicted below in the factor-cluster format.

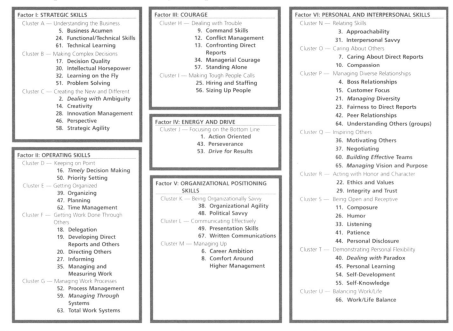

The competency requirements for any job will come from a list or library like the one above. The number of competencies required depends upon the level and complexity of the job. The number ranges from the low teens to about 30. Generally, we recommend focusing on five to seven competencies in a single interview. The 67 competencies are intended to cover the complete range of levels, functions, and responsibilities; only a portion will make a critical difference for a particular job. Some jobs may load high on particular factors and clusters; others will sample from points across the library.

What Competencies Do I Interview For?

The absolute fact of the competency interviewing approach is if you don't have the right competencies, nothing else matters. The first step in picking the right competencies is building a job profile.

In most organizations, the competencies have already been selected. Most of the critical jobs will have been analyzed. The only remaining task is to distribute the required competencies among the interviewers.

The analysis is a fairly straightforward process (Lombardo & Eichinger, 2004). The basic steps are as follows:

- **Gather a panel of six to ten subject-matter experts.** This may include current and past incumbents, bosses, and members of HR or recruiting. Ideally, you want a panel of individuals who have a keen understanding of what competencies are most critical to a particular job and who are high performers.

- **Discuss the current and future challenges/demands of the position.** This includes discussing deliverables and expectations, contributions to strategic goals, and what differentiates high performers in the job.

- **Capture the critical outcomes for the role.** From the previous discussion, determine "We need someone in this role who accomplishes _____."

- **Determine the skills or capabilities most important for meeting the critical outcomes.** Have the group determine "In order for someone to accomplish _____, we need him/her to be able to _____."

- **Sort competencies based on importance to success in the job.** Leverage the discussions above to identify the specific competencies for success. Adding structure to the sort helps. Using Lominger's competency library shown above, we recommend sorting the 67 competencies into the top 22 that are essential, the middle 23 that are nice to have, and the bottom 22 that are less important.

- **Tally results from individual raters and reach consensus on the top set of competencies.** With some luck, you may have a clear list of important competencies, but some tie breaking and reassessments are likely.

The above process would identify the top 22 competencies for the position you are hiring for.

You could at this point have a number of people conducting interviews to split up the 22 most important competencies.

You could trim the list a bit by applying a screen to the profile. The screen separates the list into price-of-admission competencies and differentiating competencies.

Price-of-admission competencies are tied to performance for the job in question, but most people tend to be good at them by the time they become candidates for this job. Examples are listed below:

• Action Oriented	• Customer Focus	• Decision Quality
• Drive for Results	• Functional/Technical Skills	• Integrity and Trust
• Intellectual Horsepower	• Learning on the Fly	• Perseverance
• Problem Solving	• Standing Alone	• Total Work Systems (e.g., Six Sigma)

You want your employees in this job to have some of these price-of-admission skills. They comprise the core of getting things done, doing them well, and showing some character in the process. It makes sense that you would want to select for these skills.

Differentiating competencies have two requirements. They are important for this job (they are on the list of 22), but few candidates for this job have them before they enter the job.

Differentiating competencies might be things like:

- Conflict Management
- Delegation
- Motivating Others
- Strategic Agility

- Creativity
- Innovation Management
- Patience
- Understanding Others

- Dealing with Ambiguity
- Listening Skills
- Personal Learning

These examples of differentiating competencies frequently appear on job profiles; however, many candidates entering these types of jobs will not be good at these competencies.

Most job profiles of the top 22 competencies are usually a 50/50 combination of price-of-admission and differentiating competencies. Best to interview for the differentiating ones.

Additional Steps in Interview Preparation

Beyond the considerations of what to interview for, here are some other things to follow or keep in mind when preparing for the interview:

- **Review the relevant job documentation.** If a job analysis and/or a detailed job description are available, spend some time looking them over to get reacquainted with the specific tasks and requirements of the role.

- **Discuss the position with key stakeholders.** In particular, you want to make sure that everyone shares an understanding of what competencies are essential for the job, how the competencies are defined, and their impact on performance.

- **Clarify roles and responsibilities with other interviewers.** If multiple people are interviewing the candidate, check that everyone clearly understands the purpose of his or her interview and what he/she will contribute to discussions of the candidate's qualifications.

It All Begins With the Right Competencies

One of the most beneficial aspects of using the Lominger library is the method for defining the requirements of the job and the most important competencies. Hiring managers generally have a good idea of what functions the position will perform. Less clear is what competencies are most important to be successful in performing the functions. When star performers are included in defining the competencies for the job, managers hear a more well-rounded perspective of what it really takes to be successful in a particular role.

I recently facilitated an exercise to define the job requirements and competencies for a new position in our sales organization. The new role would support two managers as well as a group of sales staff. As we worked through the responsibilities, it was clear the managers had not spent enough time determining specifically what this role would be responsible for, let alone what a successful candidate would "look like." As we worked through the exercise to bubble up the most needed competencies, I listened to the group disagree, persuade, explain, justify, and finally agree on what the candidate needed to succeed in this role. I was a little concerned the group might get impatient with the process. After we completed the exercise and all were satisfied that "we nailed it," I asked them how they felt about the process. The response was overwhelmingly positive. What I didn't realize was that they made an expensive mistake three months ago—hiring the wrong person, whom they had to let go. They were highly motivated to do it right this time around.

– Marilyn Westmas

- **Review the candidate's background information.** Confine this to reviewing some basic facts from the resume so you have a context for understanding the candidate's responses. We recommend against looking at data such as test scores, ratings from previous interviewers, etc. Research has shown that such data has a biasing effect on interviewers' perceptions (Campion, Palmer, & Campion, 1997). The degree to which this affects the validity of those perceptions has not been determined. Until we know this, it's better to keep things clean and simple.

- **Study designated competencies, questions, and behavioral indicators.** We will talk more about the content of the interview in the next chapter. For now, recognize the importance of taking time to study the competencies you are focusing on and develop a clear picture of the behaviors you will be looking for in the interview.

- **Schedule appropriate interview length**. Using our system, it can take approximately 10 minutes to walk through a series of questions and probes for a particular competency. Multiply this by the five to seven competencies you will likely be including in the interview, and it becomes apparent that you should schedule at least an hour in order to ask your questions and still leave a small amount of time for other conversation with the candidate.

- **Select a neutral location, if possible**. This avoids "turf issues" for either side and creates a more focused environment. Some of our best interviews have taken place in airport meeting facilities—just you and the candidate, usually quiet surroundings, and plenty of coffee right in the room.

- **Eliminate distractions**. This is an obvious one, but how many interviews do get interrupted by phone calls, instant message pop-ups, or even occasional passersby?

- **Leave time to get mentally prepared**. The interview process we have designed is fairly rigorous and can take a lot of mental stamina. It's best to take a few moments to relax, clear your head of other thoughts, and get ready to tackle the task at hand. Strongly introverted types who may find themselves even physically worn out by the interview process might find this step particularly valuable.

- **Prepare introductory remarks**. Take a few moments at the beginning to orient the candidate to the structured interview process. This frames the candidate's expectations and sets a tone for the remainder of the conversation.

Before We Begin...

Prepared introductory remarks reduce the tendency for an interviewer to ramble (sometimes saying too much about the job or competencies) and ensure that each candidate in a pool hears exactly the same opening explanation. We use the following opening comments:

During the interview, I'll be asking questions about your experiences. I'm particularly interested in HOW you did what you did and WHY you did it that way. I'll also ask about what you learned from those experiences and how you used those lessons in other situations. Please take your time in answering. I'll be taking notes so I accurately record your experiences. Do you have any questions?

– Linda Hodge

- **Anticipate questions.** This reduces the chances of getting thrown off guard during the interview. A clear, to-the-point answer helps keep the process on track.

- **Scope out next steps.** At some point during the interview the candidate is likely to ask, "What's next?" Having a straight answer helps reduce candidate anxiety and also indicates a clearly mapped-out process.

Myths and Misperceptions – Part I

Because we are human, our perceptions of people and situations are not always on the mark. Fortunately, we have been able to identify many of the biases that affect us and have also learned to minimize their impact. Despite the safeguards a structured interviewing approach puts into place, these biases are bound to pop up from time to time. By being aware of what they are, you can more easily spot them in yourself and others and limit their influence.

We also want to draw your attention to some of the persistent myths that lead people astray when assessing candidates and making decisions.

We'll highlight these myths and misperceptions as they relate to the different stages of the interview process. Here are some things to keep in mind as you are preparing for the interview:

Myth—Top past performance predicts future performance. There is an often repeated statement: "The best predictor of future behavior is past behavior." This is a reliable assumption in a limited way only—if the person is being hired for the exact same set of responsibilities that he or she had in his/her previous job. Unless the expectations and the demands of the environment are alike, a different set of competencies will be needed for success. There may be some significant overlap, but don't bet on it. Past behavior does indicate patterns—always works hard in whatever they do—but being able to be strategic in one setting and under one set of circumstances doesn't mean they will be particularly good in another.

Myth—The "right" work experience makes a qualified candidate. True, experiences can have a powerful shaping force on competency development. But the experience itself is not enough. The individual needs to have also acquired some significant lessons from the experience and had the opportunity to apply and refine those lessons in different situations. Experience is a good indicator, but its relevance to the individual needs to be probed more carefully.

Myth—They came from a top/bottom school/company. Poor employees can come from world-class companies and superstars can emerge from bottom-rung competitors. The same reasoning applies to educational credentials and lineage. In the end, it all comes down to the individual and what he or she took away from past experiences, good or bad.

22

There is a tendency among interviewers to be influenced by the fact that a candidate may have other job offers. This information is interpreted as evidence that the candidate is very high quality. In a two-part laboratory study (with one using college students and the other using professional recruiters) it was shown that, all other qualities being equal, a candidate's status as hard-to-get (e.g., considering other job opportunities) versus easy-to-get (e.g., not considering other opportunities) positively influenced the interviewers' judgments of candidate credentials and likely job offer. Therefore, don't be so quick to view a candidate as better qualified than other candidates simply because he or she has more offers on the table—pay closer attention to the candidate's actual qualifications.

– Michael A. Campion

Reference: Williams, K.B., Radefeld, P.S., Binning, J.F., & Sudak, J.R. (1993).

Misperception—"I heard this person is a great candidate." Be very mindful of hearsay. Once it has passed your ears, it will create an immediate expectation and an innate desire to search for confirming evidence. If the candidate has passed through the initial stages of selection, it's reasonable to expect that he or she comes to the table with some positive skills, but do your best to stay objective and operate with a clean slate. If you feel that others are starting to tell you too much about a candidate, politely ask them to hold on to their comments until after the interview.

Preparing Yourself

A final task is making sure you feel personally prepared to tackle the entire interview process. You'll be better able to make this judgment after you have read the remaining chapters of this book, but if you feel you need more education and practice, seek out ways to get it. A good source is within your own company. Chances are that someone has the unofficial position of "interview guru." Seek out this person as a potential mentor. Perhaps the guru will allow you to sit in on his or her interviews and/or shadow your own. Even if you are a relatively experienced interviewer, find opportunities to continue learning and get feedback on your skills. Formal interview training is another consideration. Interviewer training has been positively related to interview validity (Huffcutt & Woehr, 1999).

Now we'll tackle the interview itself. The interview is a dialog. At the heart of the dialog is the quality of the questions and the information available in the answers. The goal is to spend as little time as possible asking the questions and as much time as possible listening to the answers and gleaning their meaning.

You know the competencies you are focusing on in the interview; now you need to ask the right questions to get the information to evaluate them. As with picking competencies, multiple considerations go into formulating the questions you need to ask.

Most of the work in determining what to ask has already been done for you. There are many catalogs of questions you can purchase and use. Experts have determined exactly what questions you need to ask for each skill or competency. That aside, let's look at how they got there.

Looking for the Evidence

You have to go back to the competencies you are evaluating. Study the definitions closely. Form a clear idea of what you will be looking for. What evidence could the candidate offer that would convince you he has demonstrated that competency successfully in the past? Also look at the experiences that help shape the development of the competency. How would one learn this skill? Tapping into these experiences in the interview often allows a good opportunity to see how a candidate has applied and developed a particular competency.

Whether you are creating questions from scratch or drawing from an existing question catalog, several characteristics differentiate more effective and less effective questions:

Open or closed? Is the question more open-ended or closed-ended? Open-ended questions, those beginning with "how" or "why" or "tell me about," solicit more information. The more information you get, the better your chances of an accurate assessment. Closed-ended questions (i.e., "Did you enjoy working with your team members?" "Was it difficult to get feedback from your boss?") can end up as merely yes or no answers. On a related note, questions that focus on behaviors versus facts are also more informative. "How do you deal with the challenge of managing a large team?" is a potentially more valuable question than "What is the largest number of people you have managed?"

Real or hypothetical? Two types of questions focus on behavior—what the candidate really did or would do. Past-behavior questions draw on the candidate's actual experiences ("How *did* you influence your boss to go in a different direction?"). Situational questions ask the candidate to describe her actions under hypothetical circumstances ("How *would* you influence your boss to go in a different direction?"). Studies have found both types of questions to be valid when used as part of a structured interview process. Head-to-head comparisons have not conclusively shown which approach is better, but some recent studies have favored the past-behavior approach (e.g., Taylor & Small, 2002). Situational questions are a good test of a candidate's abstract thinking skills, but they are not a realistic measure of how that person may actually act in that situation. It is one thing to identify the appropriate course of action and another to follow it or execute it effectively. Past-behavior questions take you inside the actual thought process and actions of the candidate when faced with a real challenge. Furthermore, you can also learn what the candidate took away from the experience and how those insights were applied in other situations. Hypothetical questions do not yield these advantages.

What is the complexity of the question? Nothing is more frustrating to an interviewer than to get a blank stare (we affectionately call these "brain freezes") or the response of "I don't understand the question." Questions have to be formatted so they are as clear and direct as possible. They also have to pertain to experiences that are accessible to the candidate and solicit meaningful responses. A question framed too broadly ("How have you built a team?") might result in a diffuse response that doesn't pertain well to the competency being examined. Go too narrow ("How have you built a cross-functional team that was responsible for making process improvements during a turnaround phase?") and only a subset of candidates can relate. Somewhere in the middle is usually best ("How have you built a team with diverse backgrounds and interests?"). Finally, consider that some candidates, especially college recruits or people early in their careers, may have little actual work experience to describe. Formulate some questions that allow candidates to draw off of relevant nonwork experiences such as charity involvement, sports teams, school projects, or family issues.

26

How focused is the question? The best questions are clearly stated and have a single focus. Multi-part questions ("…and then tell me…") and questions with multiple subjects ("How did you convince your boss and your peers to adopt your strategy?") can be unnecessarily difficult for the candidate to process, and the answers are often more challenging for the interviewer to evaluate. Don't feel compelled to try to extract maximum information from a candidate with a single question. Ask a question that gets the conversation rolling and then follow up with successive probes. We'll talk more about probes in the next section.

Is the question appropriate? You might be chuckling at this right now. You might be thinking, "Of course I know which questions not to ask." Hopefully that is the case, but rest assured someone else out there doesn't know or maybe has the wrong idea. The U.S. federal guidelines on employment-related questions are very specific. It is unlawful for interviewers to ask questions that lead directly or indirectly to answers regarding an individual's race, color, religion, sex, national origin, age, marital/family status, or mental/physical abilities. Beyond that, certain state or local restrictions might also apply. Check with your HR administrator for more clarification. In instances not covered by the above, use your common sense when seeking candidates' personal information. If you have to think twice before asking the question, don't ask it. The safest bet is to concentrate in areas that are mission critical to the performance of the job.

That just covers the guidelines for basic behavioral questions. Oftentimes you will want or need to go beyond the initial question to gain more information and insight. That's where choosing the right probes comes in.

Probing for Meaning

Asking follow-up probes gets you more information and sometimes information with deeper meaning. Probing is more than prompting the candidate with "Tell me more." Probes need to provoke thought and reflection, not just extra layers of detail. In keeping with our emphasis on structure, probes should also follow a consistent form.

We have put together a series of five probe categories that can be applied to almost any situation you ask a candidate about. These probes go beyond a surface description of an event and shed more insight on the candidate's actions, thought process, and short- and long-term reactions to what happened. The initial question provides you with valuable context, a starting point, but the probes give you a clearer, more fine-grained understanding of how this individual has applied the competency in question. They also highlight strengths and opportunities for development.

Here are the five probe categories and what each taps into:

- **Actions:** How did you approach it?
- **Thinking:** Why did you select that approach?
- **Outcome:** What was the result?
- **Learnings:** What did you take away from the experience?
- **Application:** How have you used those lessons in a different situation?

The first three probes are fairly straightforward and help you understand the candidate's thoughts and behaviors in a situation:

The **Actions** probe essentially tells you more about what the candidate did. This is a good opportunity to pick up on actual behaviors related to the competency you are evaluating. If the competency in question is Planning, is there evidence that the candidate broke a larger task into individual steps and developed accurate time frames, or was there just a rush to take action and a failure to estimate the resources needed to get the job done? Listen closely for specifics.

The **Thinking** probe provides you with more information about the candidate's thought process. The candidate likely had many options to pursue in a given situation. Why was a particular approach chosen? What was the reasoning? Were alternatives considered? Responses here shed light on the actions described in the previous probe. The extent to which the candidate's reasoning is revealed also tells you whether the actions were deliberate and understood or whether they sprung from instinct or were even the product of sheer luck. The depth and style of reasoning tells you more about how the candidate actually grasps the meaning of the competency and intends to apply it. To the extent that the candidate's thinking was flawed or incomplete, you may have some early indications of needs for development.

The **Outcome** probe brings some closure to the situation being described. It is surprising how often a candidate will describe a particular action and not offer what actually happened as a result. For instance, consider the statement, "I decided to cut our workforce by 15% to cut costs and improve efficiency." By all indications the individual's move was gutsy, decisive, and bottom-line oriented. But were the cost and efficiency objectives actually achieved? What was the impact on morale and communication? The point here is not to catch the candidate in grandstanding or fabrication. Rather, the scope and depth of the response can indicate the individual's ability to recognize short- and long-term ramifications as well as gauge the impact of his or her actions on other people. These responses give insight into how well the candidate understands the competency and can apply it skillfully.

The last two probes, **Learnings** and **Application**, deserve special focus and attention. Together, they address the "so what?" factor. They also give insight into an important characteristic we call learning agility. Learning agile individuals excel at developing needed skills under challenging, first-time conditions. Furthermore, they then apply the lessons they have acquired from their past experiences in different and future situations. The ability to learn in a fluid manner, acquire multiple lessons, and make connections to new experiences is a talent that few individuals possess to a high degree. Our research and experience show that learning agility is evenly distributed among the population, forming the familiar bell-shaped curve of ability. Learning agility is also independent of IQ and personality (Connolly & Viswesvaran, 2002).

Learning agile employees are particularly valuable to the organization. Higher levels of learning agility are significantly related to future potential (Lombardo & Eichinger, 2000). Learning agile individuals perform better in promotions than non-learning-agile individuals because they more rapidly acquire necessary skills and adapt lessons from their previous experiences to the new situation. Their adaptability also guards them against derailment. Learning agile individuals are the primary talent pool for the organization's group of high potential employees and can emerge as future leaders.

The following characteristics separate more agile and less agile learners:

Less Agile Learners	More Agile Learners
Takes the path of least resistance	Likes challenges
Closed/internal processor	Open to ideas of others
General	Specific/detailed
Narrow in interests/resources	Many interests/resources
Avoids risks; waits; prefers staying the same	Accepts personal risks; takes the lead in first-time situations
Cautious	Energetic; experimental; high drive
Closed; low interest in feedback	Asks for feedback; seeks improvement
Focuses on "what" answers and solutions	Focuses on why and how; new approaches
Planful; follows steps and process	Resourceful; gets it done somehow
Lives in the present	Comfortable projecting into the future
Doesn't spot underlying patterns	Detects essence
Can't explain ideas/concepts well	Makes the complex understandable
Likes his/her personal solutions	Helps others think things through

29

The two learning agility oriented probes (Learnings and Application) allow you to evaluate the candidate's ability in both the broad and specific sense. Responses to probes about a specific situation will give you an idea of the individual's capacity for learning and adaptability for a particular competency. A broader pattern of learning agility will also form across all of the situational responses. The list of characteristics above can be used as a checklist to evaluate the candidate's overall learning agility. Since most people are moderate in learning agility, many candidates will demonstrate a mix of agile and non-agile characteristics.

The nature of the response to each of the learning agility probes also has significance. The Learnings probe offers direct insight into what the individual took away from an experience. The key things to listen for here are principles and rules-of-thumb—the more that are named, the better. Also listen for specific and/or unique insights that go beyond clichés and aphorisms.

If the Learnings probe measures the relative "input" that a person acquires from experiences, the Application probe helps you gauge the "output" factor. Occasionally individuals will identify multiple learnings from a situation, but will not necessarily repeat them in similar circumstances or make connections to different situations. Don't be quick to judge high input/low output learners as stubborn or somehow blocked; they may just lack sufficient experience or opportunity to apply what they have learned.

The Proof Is in the Probes

While the last two probes—"What did you learn?" and "How have you used those learnings in other situations?"—sound like simple questions, they are the most complex of the five probes. Remember that some people learn more from experiences than others, and it's not related to their intelligence. Learnings are generally expressed as principles or rules. For example, "I learned that the best solution is not always the first one," or "I learned that you need to break an impasse by calling a time out so people can collect their thoughts." A rich experience often yields three or more learnings or lessons.

The final probe—"How have you used those learnings in other situations?"—is often the most difficult to answer. It's not uncommon for a candidate to respond by saying he or she uses the lessons all the time, in all types of situations. While that may be the case, it's impossible to evaluate the output or application without a specific example. If the candidate responds in a very general manner, ask him or her to take some time and try to think of a specific event.

– Linda Hodge

Together, the probes form a cohesive system with its own internal logic. Practiced effectively, the probes result in answers that are thought provoking for the candidate and revealing for the interviewer.

Sticking With the Process

The probing process needs to be applied accurately and consistently to yield its full benefit. Learning the probes and knowing when and how to ask them can sometimes pose a challenge for individuals with limited exposure to structured interviewing. Here are a few tips for getting grounded in the approach:

- **Study:** Even though there are only five probes, take time to commit them to memory. Forming a note-taking template with prompts for each probe also helps. Rehearse when and how you would deliver the probes to a candidate. Engage in some practice sessions with coworkers or even family members. Observe someone who is comfortable with using the probes and extracts good answers from candidates.

- **Standardize:** Practice asking the *same* questions and probes in the *same* order to a group of candidates for the *same* position. Doing so will reinforce structure and strengthen the validity of your approach. You will also gain comfort with the flow of delivering the probes and prompting the candidate's thinking. Finally, comparing candidates will be easier since they all experienced the same set of circumstances.

- **Stay within the lines:** Seeking clarification or more specificity on a point is one thing; otherwise, try to resist the temptation to ask extra probes. If you are eager to dig for something more, chances are that what you are looking for will come out in subsequent probes. Additional probes can also knock the candidate off track and make it more difficult to resume the flow of the interview.

Once you have spent some time with the probes and seen the value they bring to the process, they won't seem as mechanical or confining. Besides, some situations call for breaking out of business-as-usual; we'll discuss these next.

Adapting to Circumstances

Candidates do not always do what you expect. Just when you think you've seen it all, something new will come up to surprise you. Interviewers need to be ready to respond to the unexpected in order to maintain their composure and sustain the flow of the interview. Here are a few prescriptions for when candidates throw you a curve:

31

- **The candidate gets stuck.** Earlier we mentioned brain freezes. These often occur in the early stages of the interview while the candidate is acclimating to the process. These periods of silence are often uncomfortable, even embarrassing, for candidates. Try to make it easy on them. Wait patiently for a moment or two. Calmly check their facial expressions for signs of an approaching answer. If they still seem stuck, interject with something like, "Don't worry. Sometimes an example is difficult to come up with. Take your time. Would you like me to repeat the question?" Usually that will do the trick.

- **The candidate is long-winded.** Verbose candidates are especially troublesome when time is limited. How can you learn about their different experiences and abilities if they are still stuck on their first example after 20 minutes? Sometimes this is a by-product of initial interview jitters. But if that doesn't seem like the case, then early intervention is needed. Politely interject; briefly summarize what the candidate has described and quickly transition to your next probe or main question. It may be necessary to do this more than once to establish the right tone and flow for the conversation.

- **The candidate keeps using the same example.** Sometimes candidates have a singular positive or negative experience that shapes much of their career and development. As such, they often want to relate their lessons from this experience in the interview. This is all very good, but what if the candidate has chosen to learn just from this one experience and everything is minimized by comparison? That could be the sign of a blocked learner or an individual who sees his or her experiences through a narrow lens. Prompt the candidate to identify some other experiences, perhaps from a different job or outside of work altogether.

- **The candidate provides a very intriguing response.** Sometimes the Application probe will lead the candidate to describe an additional situation that captures your interest. If you want to know more and think it will add to your insights on the candidate, begin with a fresh set of probes to delve further into the candidate's experience. We call this process "chaining." This technique is a bit more advanced. You may want to consult a more experienced interviewer for some tips on when and how to use this approach.

- **The candidate gets you stuck.** That's right. Sometimes the shoe is on the other foot. A candidate may sometimes tell a story in such a way that the probe you are ready to ask needs to be amended or just doesn't fit. The general rule here is to try to paraphrase or to incorporate some of what the candidate said into your probe. Sometimes it's better and more appropriate to ask something like, "So, how did the board respond to your proposal to sell the company?" than to say, "What was the outcome?"

- **The candidate answers your probe before you ask it.** This often happens with a learning agile candidate who quickly grasps the structure and flow of the interview. Don't fret, just move past that probe to the next one you were prepared to ask.

Beyond these more common examples, we recommend keeping an informal log of how you responded to interview situations that caught you off guard or presented you with a new challenge.

Additional Tips for Conducting Interviews

Questions and probes drive much of the interview, but not everything. Here are a few other things to keep in mind during the interview:

- **Set an appropriate tone.** Setting and maintaining the right tone is critical. You want to create an environment that is comfortable to talk in but does not bias the conversation. Try to interact with the candidate in a balanced and professional manner. Listen attentively and be approachable and engaging, but strike a relatively neutral pose when it comes to being encouraging or disapproving of a candidate's responses. Watch the use of "That's interesting," "Oh, really," and "Hmmm." Be particularly careful with managing your nonverbal cues such as facial expressions. This doesn't mean you have to strip yourself of all emotion. You want the interaction to have some flow, but not to be so relaxed and informal that it interferes with the structure of the interview.

- **Clarify procedures.** As we mentioned in the previous section, prepare some introductory remarks to brief candidates on the purpose and format of the interview. This may be a new experience for the candidate. Knowing what to expect will reduce anxiety and speed up acclimating to the process. As you interview more and more candidates, you may want to go back and tweak your opening comments to correspond with frequent questions.

- **Maintain your focus.** Following the first two steps, plus reducing distractions in your environment, will help your focus considerably. Also, the better you understand what you are interviewing for and how to spot it, the more you will be able to focus in on the experience the candidate is describing and what it means.

- **Monitor the pace.** Make sure you can cover what you want in the time allotted. To speed things up, consider some of the suggestions we made for dealing with long-winded candidates. Also, selectively prefacing prompts with "Briefly tell me…" can act as a subtle cue and get the pace of the interview on track. On occasion, you may need to do the opposite and slow the candidate down a bit. This may be a product of nervousness and will gradually decrease over the course of the interview, so wait and see at first. Some candidates move quickly because they are overly general in their responses. Sometimes this is a characteristic of their personality style, other times they may have been trained to give interviewers concise answers and not divulge too much detail. Where necessary, ask for specific examples or more detailed descriptions so you gain more from the candidate's response.

- **Take notes.** Note taking is a valuable part of the interview process. For some individuals, it keeps them engaged in processing information and observations from the interview. Notes are especially helpful for maintaining a clear recollection of the interview once it's over (Middendorf & Macan, 2002). Feedback discussions with other interviewers are enriched by being able to provide a clear account of a candidate's actions in particular situations and what they meant. To avoid bogging down, we recommend taking notes in short bullet points and capturing key facts that will help keep your memory fresh.

- **Reach closure.** Conducting the interview requires you to process a lot of information in a short period of time. Note taking eases this process, but sometimes a mental pause is needed. Be careful of immediately transitioning into a separate set of questions and probes if you still have a thought stuck in your head. If you do, your focus will not be as strong to evaluate the next competency. Either keep your head focused on your notes page until your mind is clear or politely ask the candidate for a moment to jot another observation. Once you've got it down, shift your focus to the next question and proceed.

> ### Remember, This Isn't a Race
>
> Research indicates that managers and executives are typically smart, action oriented, and drive hard for results. The strengths of typical managers are virtually the opposite of what is needed to be great interviewers—patience, listening, and process management. One of the most common mistakes we see interviewers make is rushing the candidate. The interviewer appears to be on a fast-paced, fact-finding mission. He or she asks a question, checks a box, and moves on. Surface responses with little substance are accepted. Interviewing is one of the few times in business when SLOW DOWN is the right action.
>
> *– Linda Hodge*

Myths and Misperceptions – Part II

Myths dominated during the preparation phase. Now the misperceptions have their turn.

Myth—A good impression makes a good candidate. When a candidate makes a good impression, the competencies you are picking up on are likely clustered in the Personal and Interpersonal Skills factor. To the extent that competencies such as Approachability, Composure, and Listening are critical to the role, then the good impression is probably a valid indicator. However, consider whether the candidate possesses other competencies important to day-to-day performance. Carefully selecting your competencies prior to the interview and having a clear focus on the behaviors you are looking for will help guard against making this leap in logic. Recent research shows that as interview structure increases, the influence of candidates' impression management efforts decreases (Tsai, Chen, & Chiu, 2005).

Misperception—Focusing attention on the beginning and the end of the interview. Given the way our memories are formed, things that happen early or late in an interaction tend to leave the strongest impression. In behavioral science, this is called the primacy/recency effect. The events that take place and the observations that are made at the beginning and end of the interview are just as valid and important as what happens in between. Consistent note taking and a clear structure to the interview will help counter the primacy/recency effect.

35

Misperception—The halo effect. When we detect a quality in an individual that leaves a strong positive impression, we have a tendency to automatically generalize that positive impression to multiple dimensions of the person's behavior (Thorndike, 1920). If the individual has a strong drive for results, then we also expect that he/she prioritizes effectively or can make timely decisions. The same effect exists for negative behaviors. ("That person is arrogant, he must also be dishonest.") Both cases represent plausible assumptions, but they need to be verified with actual demonstrations of the related behaviors in order to make a case. Having clear criteria and paying close attention to actual behavior during the interview lessens the chance of perceiving something that isn't necessarily there.

Misperception—Attribution errors. When others do not perform up to expectations, the natural judgment is that the individual was somehow to blame; something about that person caused that outcome to occur (Jones & Davis, 1965). That may very well be the case, but seldom are external factors, including those beyond the person's control, taken into account. A clear description of the situation and insight into the individual's thought process can help clarify the why behind what happened. The Learning probes might also reveal whether or not the candidate feels personally accountable for what happened.

Misperception—Stereotypes. We are all affected by stereotypes; they help make a complex world simpler to understand. They can exert a powerful force on our perceptions and behavior. Some stereotypes take root in our worldview and never change. An effective way to combat stereotypes is to recognize which ones affect you the most. Feedback from others, while difficult, may strengthen this realization. When you feel that a stereotype may be influencing your perceptions, carefully assess whether the behaviors you observed in the candidate validate drawing the conclusions you are making.

Misperception—Similar-to-me bias. The basic theory here is that we tend to like and feel more comfortable with individuals whom we see as similar to ourselves. Differences are more difficult to understand and are therefore more threatening. It was once thought that this bias was prevalent in the interview, particularly with regard to similar experiences and shared demographics. Recent research suggests that these effects aren't as strong as previously thought. However, it appears that similarities in attitudes may positively influence perceptions (Posthuma, Morgeson, & Campion, 2002).

The Fundamental Attribution Error

The bias in how people explain the successes and failures of themselves compared to others is so common that it has become known as the "Fundamental" Attribution Error. Research has shown that this error occurs in a wide range of work and other life contexts.

Fundamental Attribution Error		
	How We Explain Ourselves	How We Explain Others
For Success	• I worked hard. • I am competent.	• They got lucky. • The task was easy.
For Failure	• I got unlucky. • The task was difficult.	• They did not work hard. • They are not competent.

This error is so ironic that it almost seems funny. However, it is so pervasive and important that its influence on important work-related decisions should not be underestimated, especially in the interview context.

– Michael A. Campion

Classic reference: Jones, E.E., & Harris, V.A. (1967).
Recent review: Gilbert, D.T., & Malone, P.S. (1995).

Misperception—Attractiveness. The attractiveness bias often receives a lot of attention in the media. Despite the number of studies in this area, results are suggestive but not conclusive (Posthuma, Morgeson, & Campion, 2002). The indication is that perceptions of attractive individuals appear reasonably valid, but can also be slightly inflated across the board. In other words, an attractive person might indeed be a good planner, negotiator, and strategist, but not quite as strong as we perceive him or her.

Take a quick look back over the list you just read. Mark areas that are real or potential weak spots. Determine what you might be able to do to lessen or avoid their impact during the interview. Stay on guard for when your potential weak spots might be influencing your perceptions. During the evaluation and decision-making phase that takes place following the interview, pay attention to whether others are being influenced by misperceptions. Constructively challenge them and probe for clear evidence that supports their perceptions.

Summarizing your observations, evaluating the candidate, and making the decision is a challenging ending to the interview process. It's where the real return on investment is determined. Making the right decision, pro or con, is where the money counter starts.

Coming to a Conclusion Based Upon Information From the Interview(s)

Does the candidate have the competency you were interviewing for? To help guide your thought and decision process, we have defined a set of behaviors or signs consistent with a candidate who either probably has or does not have the competency under consideration. These positive and negative themes, or "look-fors," are not meant to be an exhaustive list of behaviors that define the competency, just a representative sample to use as a guideline. If you choose to use an existing system, look for one that has a catalog of competencies, questions, probes, and look-fors.

Here is a sample of look-fors for Quality of Decision Making:

Con or Negative Themes	Pro or Positive Themes
(1) Makes quick decisions without analysis	(1) Objectively gathers information
(2) Relies too much on self and close-in information	(2) Knows priorities
(3) Lack of clear issue definition	(3) Identifies key factors/themes in the definition
(4) Not orderly in thinking	(4) Thorough question and consideration of the nature of the decision
(5) Feelings play too large a role	(5) Defines issues/problems clearly; sought out for advice by others
	(6) (Overuse) Perfectionist, has overriding need to be right; analyzes excessively

Note the Overuse category (number 6). The expression of a competency ranges from doing none of it, some of it, about as much as most people do (middle or average), to doing more than most, to doing a lot of it well. On the high end, it's also possible to spill into doing it too much. That's called overuse. The competency goes into overdrive. It's overdone. Even though the person does a lot of it, it becomes potentially negative by doing too much of it. Being very funny is probably a skill a lot of people would like to have. It's also possible to be too funny in the wrong situations, to make light of very serious topics, or to spend too much time being funny when others want to get to the work at hand. When a competency is overused or taken too far, it can have a negative impact.

We'll talk a little more about the role of look-fors when we discuss making candidate ratings. First, we want to highlight some other techniques and strategies for evaluating candidates.

> ### The Importance of Sticking to the Script
>
> The five positive and five negative themes are linked to the main questions. The themes were selected based on what an interviewer would most likely be able to hear or observe in an interview setting. Because the questions and themes are connected, changing the main questions can impact the themes. Therefore, try to use the questions as they were originally written.
>
> *– Linda Hodge*

15 Tips for Evaluating Candidates

We recognize that some of the tips included below are also relevant to what takes place during the interview. We include them in this section to emphasize that evaluating what takes place during the interview doesn't stop when the interview is over. Evaluating and making sense of what the candidate did and said is an ongoing process.

(1) **Keep an open mind.** This prescription is simple in concept, but not always easy to follow. Using a structured process with follow-up probes requires a certain degree of patience. As you progress through the probes and learn more about the candidate's experience, your perceptions may change. Also keep in mind that the question you ask may prompt the candidate to recall a negative experience. Perhaps the candidate did not apply the competency effectively in that particular instance, but also give fair consideration to what was learned from the experience. Did the candidate recognize how to improve? Did subsequent situations demonstrate more awareness and

a better mastery of the competency? You also need to keep an open mind to the entire process, not just the responses to individual questions. Some candidates show a spark at the beginning of the interview that gradually fades; others start out on a weak foot and steadily gain strength. Keep monitoring and consider the whole, not just particular parts that stand out in your attention.

(2) **Weigh data appropriately.** Try to look at positive and negative observations objectively. If you find yourself responding (positive or negative) to things the candidate did or said, try to step away and get some distance from your observations before reaching a final conclusion. As a result, you may gain a better understanding as to *why* you initially responded to the candidate that way. This will allow you to make a better informed evaluation. Most untrained interviewers give too much weight to negative information.

(3) **Consider opportunities for development.** If you perceive that a candidate does not effectively demonstrate or apply a competency, what are the chances that the candidate's performance could be strengthened with the right learning experiences and coaching? Consider the development resources your organization has available and how people who would work closely with the candidate could help. Remember, some competencies can be developed more easily and in a shorter period of time. Many pathways can be taken to development (Eichinger, Lombardo, & Stiber, 2005).

(4) **Align your observations with the competency.** Sometimes "conceptual confusion" occurs when evaluating competencies. For example, you might be rating a candidate on Planning skills, but the observations you are basing your judgment on are actually more akin to Organizing. As a safeguard against this, always refer back to definitions and look-fors and make certain that your perceptions are focused where you want them to be.

(5) **Consider what isn't said.** Sometimes what a candidate doesn't do is as important as what he or she does do. The absence of thoughts, behaviors, or information you would otherwise expect to pick up on may be indicative of an underdeveloped competency. The Actions and Thinking probes can reveal some noteworthy gaps in the candidate's approach. Be careful not to leap to conclusions, though. Chaining through other situations to see if you observe the same gaps might provide some reinforcement for your initial perceptions.

(6) **Evaluate the broader context.** Behaviors don't exist in a vacuum. Take a look at the big picture and see how elements of the environment may be having an influence. This also helps lessen the impact of attribution errors.

41

(7) **Pay attention to past and present behaviors.** Thus far, we have focused on evaluating the candidate's past behaviors. Don't forget those that are right in front of you. The interview provides a great forum for directly observing a number of competencies such as Listening, Approachability, Composure, Self-Knowledge, and Learning on the Fly. Make sure to integrate what you are observing in real time with your perceptions of past actions.

(8) **Predicting the future.** In a sense, you are taking the impressions you have collected in the interview and are predicting what this person may or may not do in the real job. You have to project the candidate's past and present behaviors into on-the-job situations and weigh the potential impacts.

(9) **Take note of other relevant behaviors.** Don't limit yourself to scanning for look-fors; they capture only a subset of behaviors related to a competency. Carefully study the definition of the competency and learn to recognize how it surfaces in different situations.

(10) **Look for patterns and themes.** Look for opportunities to connect the dots in your understanding of a candidate's behavior. Evidence of how an individual performs on a particular competency may occur across a number of situations the candidate describes. For example, you might be asking a question about Conflict Management, but the candidate's experience also relates to some of the insights you made earlier when you were focused on evaluating Perseverance. Patterns can also be detected in how competencies interact with one another. For instance, a candidate's high Drive for Results combined with low Patience might contribute to being pushy toward direct reports and others.

(11) **Don't ignore the obvious.** Sometimes towering strengths or glaring weaknesses of the candidate emerge that were not part of your original focus for the interview. Don't ignore these incidental observations. Take note of them and consider their importance to job performance.

(12) **Consider your own tendencies/biases.** We cautioned earlier about the impact of stereotypes and other types of misperceptions. Beyond these, pay attention to some of the other mental frameworks you carry into the interview. In particular, many of us develop an image of the ideal candidate in our minds (Webster, 1964). This is helpful for training your observations during the interview, but can also spark some dangers. First, be realistic in your expectations and recognize that you will seldom find the

ideal candidate—everyone has shortcomings. Also, realize that behaviors that fall outside of your ideal definition aren't necessarily negative; those behaviors might be very valuable, they just don't correspond to your ideal.

(13) **Account for ambiguities.** Ambiguity comes with the territory when you interview candidates. Loose ends in your observations are inevitable. Try your best to fill in the blanks when and where you can. Look for trends in how the candidate evaluated situations, made decisions, and took action. If you have limited information to draw from, try checking your gut to see what your intuition is telling you.

(14) **Attempt to reconcile discrepancies and contradictions.** Occasionally something the candidate says arouses either confusion or suspicion on your part. File away your impression and see if you can gather any other information to clarify or confirm it. In some circumstances, you may gather sufficient evidence that the candidate is pushing the envelope on impression management. More likely, either nervousness or lazy thinking can lead to misstatements.

(15) **Leave sufficient time to conduct your evaluation.** Even if you are extremely busy and have a cramped schedule, do whatever you can to avoid rushing through this stage of the interview process. Take time to reflect on the observations you made and perceptions you formed during the interview. Review your notes. Pose questions to yourself. Let your thoughts incubate. Engaging in this process will help you make accurate judgments and reinforce your confidence in whatever decision you make on the candidate.

Making Ratings

Several smaller judgments influence a final rating on a competency. First, consider the positive and negative behavioral themes you observed in the candidate's responses. For many candidates, you will have identified a mixture of positives and negatives. Resist the temptation to add up the number of positives and the number of negatives, see which is greater, and then tilt your rating in that direction. The behaviors you observed need to be looked at objectively and weighed against one another. Consider which ones will really have an impact on that person's performance in the job.

Next, refer back to the definition for the competency.

- What behaviors consistent with the competency did you observe that were not part of the behavioral themes?

- Were they positive or negative?

- How are they likely to influence the candidate's performance?

Finally, reflect on your experiences interviewing other people on this competency as well as observing it in your coworkers.

- How does this person compare to others?

- More specifically, how does the candidate compare to other people who have been incumbents in the role?

The more data points you have collected and sorted out, the more easily and precisely you can judge the candidate's overall strength on a competency.

Each of these considerations will combine to inform your choice of a rating, usually a number somewhere between 1 and 5. Don't feel pressured to make a final rating immediately. We recommend making a preliminary rating during the course of the interview and then going back to check it following the meeting. In many cases, you will settle with your initial rating. On some occasions, your evaluation process may lead you to reconsider and shift your rating slightly. If you find yourself making ratings shifts greater than one point, say from a 4 to a 2, exercise some caution and make sure you can justify both your initial and final ratings.

While the candidate's ability to demonstrate competencies critical to the job is an important consideration in making a hiring decision, it needs to be evaluated along with other criteria. Summary ratings can be made on the competencies you interviewed for as well as on other candidate characteristics. Categories to be rated might include the following:

- Experience, Past Performance, and Track Record

- Job/Functional/Technical Skills

- Organization/Culture Fit

- Competencies You Specifically Interview For

- Other Competencies You Observed During the Interview

- Learning Agility

Be careful to rate only the categories where you have gathered an adequate amount of information and can clearly justify your conclusions. If you are unable to make a rating but still have some relevant observations to offer to others, record these and save them for the information-sharing session.

Sharing Perceptions and Making Decisions

If you are making a hiring decision solely on your own, then you need to weigh the various factors you rated. If you interviewed multiple candidates, then you will also need to make comparisons to determine the most qualified person.

Chances are that you will be working with several other people to reach a hiring decision. This calls for a somewhat more elaborate and formalized process. Before you even convene the decision panel, a few matters need to be settled. First, make sure the criteria for evaluating candidates are clearly communicated and understood. Next, determine how the final decision will be made. Does one individual have the final say? Is complete consensus needed? Is a simple majority sufficient? Establishing clear lines of authority and accountability will lessen opportunities for confusion, hurt feelings, and second-guessing. Finally, confirm that each panel member is clear on his or her role in the process.

Another important consideration that shouldn't be overlooked is how to weight different categories of candidate criteria (Functional/Technical Skills, Fit, Competencies, etc.). There are no clear guidelines or rules of thumb to suggest whether or not these categories should be differentially weighted, let alone which ones would deserve lower or higher weightings. It all comes down to what your organization determines matters the most. A helpful way to shape this decision is by taking a historical look at unsuccessful hiring decisions and trying to pinpoint the factors that were overlooked or not given sufficient weight that ended up being important. It could be that your organization has a history of "organ transplant rejection"—where highly talented candidates are hired who are unable to work effectively within the confines of the organization's culture. Likewise, you might be hiring people who represent the right "fit" and have the right functional/technical skills, but possess limited amounts of the competencies that are critical for success. Either way, target your areas of weakness and make sure they are adequately accounted for in the decision-making process.

Once everyone is together, the process consists of three basic steps: (1) reviewing observations, (2) integrating perceptions, and (3) making a decision. Begin by having each panel member summarize his or her impressions of the candidate with regard to the key competencies being considered. Naturally, this will include a mention of the competencies that the candidate is particularly strong in or needs to develop. Avoid the mention of specific ratings at this time so the group doesn't immediately get stuck on a number and lean toward a decision. (Let's assume for the sake of this discussion that there is overlap in the competencies that each member of the panel interviewed for. In some cases, however, specific competencies may be assigned only to a subset of individuals who have a particular expertise in assessing them; in those situations, the group should follow the individual assessor's lead in evaluating the candidate's strength on those competencies, but still be invited to add any relevant observations.)

Sorting Out What Really Matters

It's very difficult to be objective about whom you decide to hire. After all, we *are* human. Successfully using a team approach requires everyone to provide examples and supporting evidence for his or her conclusions. It also requires the team to focus its attention on how the candidate has demonstrated his or her grasp of the top priority competencies for the job and not get sidetracked by focusing on less-critical characteristics.

I recall an interview with a female candidate for one of Berbee's technical management positions. The candidate held a similar role with another consulting firm and provided ample examples from her wealth of experience that were consistent with the competencies we were looking for. In the interview debriefing, two of the interviewers (who were also female) were opposed to hiring the candidate. The other four interviewers strongly supported hiring the candidate. When pressed by the team for supporting evidence, the two women revealed that they were uncomfortable with the candidate's strong assertiveness and "overconfidence." While these observations regarding the candidate's interpersonal skills were of some potential concern, they were not seen as primary drivers of success or failure in the role as it had been defined.

Although we usually aim for consensus in hiring decisions, the other team members were so convinced of the candidate's strengths on the competencies that were deemed critical for the role that they decided to invoke the "majority opinion" and hire the candidate. Four years later we can say with confidence that the team made the right hiring decision. Her team is one of the highest-performing teams in the organization and turnover one of the lowest. Had we focused on some of the less-important behaviors for this particular role, we may have lost this person to a competitor.

– *Marilyn Westmas*

Full participation is essential for a thorough and balanced discussion of the candidate. As each member shares impressions of the candidate, other panelists should seek clarification and ask some constructive, probing questions. Discourage broad pronouncements ("This candidate has no strategic skills.") and seek appropriate justification for judgments based on what was observed during the interview. Also, keep a lookout for some of the biases we noted previously and challenge them appropriately. Sometimes a panel member will share an intuitive impression or a vague notion regarding the candidate. Rather than dismiss these, help the panelist to explore the reasoning behind these impressions and try to identify their link to specific behaviors that were observed.

At the end of the review discussion, identify emerging areas of agreement and difference that may factor into the final decision-making process. Consider whether any more discussion of differences is merited before moving on to the next phase.

Next, give everyone a moment to go back to his or her original ratings and make any adjustments based on the discussion. Then put everyone's ratings on a grid to take a look at how the ratings compare and what trends emerge. Continue the discussion and see if a consensus can be reached on how to rate the candidate in each category. Here is an example of what a typical ratings grid might look like:

Competency	Rater 1	Rater 2	Rater 3	Rater 4
Delegation	4	4	3	4
Listening Skills	4	3	4	3
Motivating Others	3	3	4	3
Strategic Agility	4	4	4	4
Understanding Others	3	3	4	5
Learning Agility	2	2	4	2

In this example, there is good convergence in the ratings with the exception of learning agility. If this hasn't been discussed extensively already, panel members should share their observations, identify the nature of their differences, and see if any agreement can be reached. Interestingly, learning agility often plays a critical role in discussing the candidate's merits. For example, a candidate with more moderate or even low ratings might be seen as having strong potential to develop based on having higher learning agility. These "diamonds in the rough" are sometimes seen as a worthwhile investment, especially if the organization possesses strong resources to aid their development. Likewise, a candidate with low learning agility and otherwise strong ratings also merits special consideration.

These individuals often function well in "High Professional" assignments that are relatively stable and draw off of a well-developed knowledge base and technical skill set.

Keep in mind that the discussion of competencies and learning agility may only represent a portion of the broader discussion of candidate qualifications. When it comes to discussing factors such as functional/technical skills or culture fit, be prepared to provide input in areas where you have been assigned a particular responsibility. Otherwise, wait to hear what others have to say in the categories they specifically evaluated and follow up with any relevant observations if you are asked. As the discussion moves to other areas of candidate qualifications and performance, weigh what is being said against the knowledge and insight you have gathered about the candidate's competencies.

You may want to construct a table similar to the following to help summarize the candidate's qualifications:

	Rating	Weight (Optional)	Qualified	Not Qualified	Comments
Credentials					
Functional / Technical Skills					
Cultural Fit					
Competencies					
Learning Agility					
Net Decision					

Once all of the information about the candidate has been put on the table and discussed, the final decision comes next. Refer back to the ground rules that were defined earlier in this chapter to guide the process. A few other considerations are in order. First, unless a single candidate is clearly superior to others, you will need to make some comparisons. It is easy to select the candidate with the highest overall scores, but often the difference between candidates with overall ratings of 4.2 and 4.3 is negligible. We cautioned earlier about making gut decisions about candidates, but it becomes more necessary at this stage of the process. Also, remember that your decision, while instinctive, is backed up by a lot of meaningful data you have gathered about the candidate.

You may have settled upon a clear winner among your candidate pool, but before you can reach a firm final decision, you also need to identify how that individual compares to the standard you have set for the position. If your top candidate is, in

> ### Beneficial Effects of Being an Interviewer
>
> Being an interviewer not only helps you hire better people, but it may make you a better manager as well. In a research study of 80 managers who were serving as assessors in an assessment center, experience as an assessor resulted in several beneficial outcomes for the assessors themselves, including:
>
> - Improved skill in interviewing and observing people to obtain relevant information.
>
> - Improved skill in verbally presenting and defending information about other people's qualifications.
>
> - Reduced error and greater accuracy in judging the behavior of others.
>
> These skills are clearly relevant to being a successful manager. As such, an extra bonus from participating in interviewing and interviewing training is the improvement of your skills as a manager.
>
> *– Michael A. Campion*
>
> *Reference: Lorenzo, R.V. (1984).*

fact, middle-of-the-road in terms of qualifications, is this really the best person? No matter what the situation, just be wary of setting the bar either too high or too low.

At this point, you're ready to make a decision. Before you make a phone call to the candidate you have selected, have a brief discussion with the panel about what might be some valuable developmental experiences for this person once he or she is on the job. Who will be in charge of that person's development? How will progress be measured? Thinking ahead to these steps will make them easier to implement when the time comes.

Following the process we laid out is fairly easy to administer, but can also require some time and energy. The effort is worth it in the end if you can make a well-justified decision and feel comfortable that you have selected the best-qualified candidate. The benefits will continue to accrue with that person's performance on the job.

Myths and Misperceptions – Part III

You're not out of the woods quite yet. A few biases can still crop up at this stage of the process:

Myth—Smarter people always make better leaders. Considerable research has shown that intelligence is a valid predictor of job performance (Hunter & Hunter, 1984). However, leadership is a complex task that involves more than just pure cognitive abilities. IQ also needs to be balanced with EQ (Goleman, 1998). Also consider that most individuals at the leadership level have at least a base level of intelligence. Because most executives share a comparable level of intellect, it does not discriminate well between good and not-so-good candidates. People skills, on the other hand, may differ widely.

Myth—The most technically qualified person, the one who knows the most about the content of the job, is the best choice for the leadership position. For many decades, individuals with a combination of the most seniority and highest level of technical skill were promoted into leadership roles. In many cases, their skills proved valuable for solving problems, and they could also be mentors to less-experienced employees. However, the abilities of technical experts to adapt to new challenges and shifting circumstances,

---

The Limited Value of Reference Checks

Although widely used, researchers have long known the limited value of reference checks for hiring. References provided by candidates tend to be characterized by leniency because most people can find someone who will say something positive about them. And contacting past supervisors or peers is often unsuccessful because most large organizations explicitly instruct employees not to provide detailed information on the job performance of former employees because of concerns over being sued for slander. The result is that reference checks tend to virtually always be positive and lacking in any useful variation, be low in reliability, and have no ability to predict future job performance. Worse yet, glowing references may be deceiving, dependent more on the reference provider than the candidate, and lead you to hire a less-qualified candidate. Some reference checking may be necessary to document basic credentials (e.g., education, past jobs, etc.) and other critical information (e.g., arrest record, citizenship, etc.), but useful information on past job performance is rarely gained.

– Michael A. Campion

Reference: Muchinsky, P.M. (1979).

50

to lead change, and to provide a compelling vision to motivate others are often overlooked. These characteristics are independent of technical skill and also need to be taken into account when evaluating a leader's potential.

Myth—They had good/bad references. References cannot be counted on as reliable sources of information. In some cases, individuals are hesitant to confirm anything beyond the basic facts about a candidate for fear that they might become the target of a lawsuit if something they say hurts a candidate's chances. Also, personal biases and hidden agendas can positively or negatively influence the referent's comments. Finally, since candidates usually nominate their references, they are likely to be individuals with a strong positive inclination toward the candidate.

Misperception—The contrast effect. Over the years, we have seen many individuals and hiring panels fall prey to this illusion. The way the contrast effect works is that after you have seen several mediocre candidates, your perceptions of an average candidate's skills can be positively inflated. After the candidate is hired, disappointment can set in when the candidate doesn't perform quite as strongly as expected. The contrast effect is well documented in behavioral science (Wexley, Yukl, Kovacs, & Sanders, 1972). The best way to combat it is to establish clear standards for evaluating candidates' responses and maintain a consistent approach through all phases of the interview.

Now you know the basics and essentials of conducting a successful interview. The remainder of the book will help you further refine your interviewing skill set.

CHAPTER 5

FOR THE ADVANCED INTERVIEWER

This chapter presents three variations (breadth, depth, and potential) on the basic model we have defined for interviewing. Each has a specific application and requires a different set of techniques. A separate book could be written about each of these approaches, so we will keep our comments here brief. If you have an interest in learning one of these interviewing styles, you can contact us for more guidance. We also recommend you seek out your organization's interviewing guru for mentoring and practice.

Interviewing for Breadth: Assessing the Whole or Complete Person

Interviewing for breadth allows you to capture a more complete picture of the candidate's overall behavioral style and skills. Taking this approach requires a stronger working knowledge of individual competencies as well as understanding how different competencies relate to and influence each other.

Interviewing to assess the whole person (all relevant competencies) is a bit ambitious. It would take too much time, and the likelihood of error increases. We recommend trimming your exploration of the candidate at the level of competency factors (Interpersonal Skills, Strategic Skills, Operational Skills, etc.) and/or clusters. This still gives you a more complete view of the candidate.

A longer interview is necessary to capture a more complete whole person assessment. A minimum of two hours is usually necessary. As many as three hours may be required. There are about five to seven factors most systems outline as being descriptive of the whole person (for our suggestions, see the factor-cluster map in Chapter 2). When conducting the interview, you need to step through questions, probes, and look-fors across all of the factors or however many you choose to cover. It takes some discipline to stick to the plan.

If you interview at the more detailed—or cluster—level, there are 20 to 30 clusters to choose from (for our suggestions, see the factor-cluster map in Chapter 2). At this level, even more discipline is required.

You need to achieve some balance in incorporating factors and clusters that are critical to performance based on the job profile you have created. Focus your attention first on trying to evaluate these key areas. At the same time, over the course of the interview, keep your eyes open to broader patterns and trends that relate to different factors and clusters.

This type of interview requires a lot of post-analysis on your part. The abilities to shift perspective, deal with ambiguity, and synthesize complex observations are all necessary to connect the dots and fill in the blanks. Start the evaluation process as you normally would by rating the areas you explored. Then look back over your factor-cluster notes and try to create some summary descriptions of the behavior patterns you observed in different areas. You may have to go back and make adjustments as your observations take shape and you make new connections. We recommend against making specific ratings on factors and clusters; even with a very rich, extensive interview, you might not have enough data collected in certain areas to justify a rating.

When you are finished, take a step back and look at how everything relates. Highlight factors and clusters where the candidate has particular strengths or developmental needs. Consider how the overall pattern will impact job performance and organization fit. Are there some key areas to leverage for development? Can the job be tweaked to better fit the candidate's profile?

External input is helpful for validating your perspective. Listen carefully to others' observations to help add texture and depth to your understanding.

Because of the time and energy needed to conduct this type of interview, you need to be able to justify your investment. Interviewing for the whole person is useful if a person is going to be "groomed" for more responsibility in the near future, in which case a more complete profile will provide added input for creating a development plan. This approach is also helpful for high-stakes roles where "no stone must be left unturned" before hiring the candidate.

Interviewing for Completeness or Depth: The Four-Dimensional Approach

This approach expands the interviewer's tool kit of techniques. Interviewing for depth involves using multiple types, or avenues, of questions and probes for the same competency. This allows you to dig deep into a particular competency and gain a very fine-grained understanding of the candidate's potential in that area.

We call this deep-dive process the four-dimensional (or 4D) approach since the competency is evaluated from four different perspectives (Lombardo & Eichinger, 2006). The focus of each perspective is illustrated below:

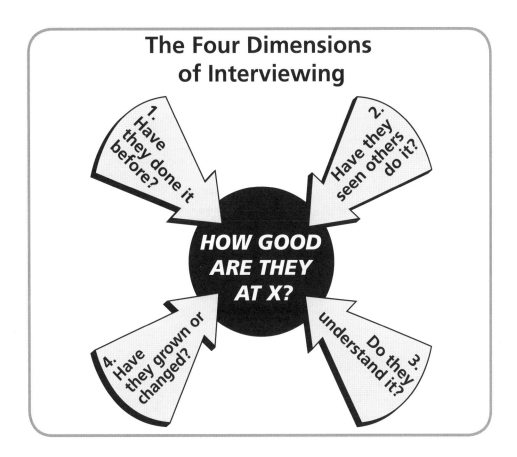

The Four Dimensions of Interviewing

1. Have they done it before?

2. Have they seen others do it?

HOW GOOD ARE THEY AT X?

3. Do they understand it?

4. Have they grown or changed?

Dimension 1 overlaps with the basic approach we have already discussed. The focus is on how the candidate has demonstrated the competency in previous situations. Dimension 1 questions begin with prompts such as:

- Tell me about a time when…   - Have you ever…

- What did you do when…   - Are there times when…

Dimension 2 taps into how much the candidate has learned from others. This includes both positive and negative role models. Observing how others approach a competency can have a strong shaping influence. Dimension 2 asks questions such as:

- Have you ever seen…   - Who is the best at…

- Who is the worst at…   - Who is a role model of…

- Have you been around someone who…

Dimension 3 assesses whether the candidate understands the competency on a more conceptual or academic level. Can the candidate articulate how the competency works for other people and for himself or herself? Dimension 3 asks questions like:

- How does ___ work?   - What happens if you are high in…

- What happens if you are low in…   - How do you develop…

Dimension 4 delves more deeply into how learning agile the candidate is in a competency. Awareness of strengths and weaknesses and efforts to develop are considered. Dimension 4 asks questions such as:

- How have you changed over your career in…

- What have been some significant learning events for you around…

- When did you make the most progress in…

Candidates' responses to the questions will result in different patterns of strengths and weaknesses across the four dimensions. Different patterns lead to different interpretations. For example, a candidate who demonstrates strength in Dimensions 2 and 3 and needs development in Dimensions 1 and 4 could be classified as someone who overestimates his or her capability and may require some firm feedback and more intensive coaching.

Careful preparation is required for a 4D interview. Questions need to be chosen that tap each dimension. Custom probes are required to follow up the primary question in each dimension. Beyond the questions and probes themselves, themes and look-fors should be tailored to each dimension.

Conducting a 4D interview also takes more time. Like interviewing for breadth, it should be reserved for situations where it will provide the most benefit. The 4D approach to interviewing is particularly effective for focusing in on a very specific set of competencies that are absolutely essential to a role. These may be competencies that are complex, difficult to master, and hard to find. You want to be sure that the candidate actually possesses them or, if not, have an idea of how to best develop them on the job.

[For more information or help in learning the 4D techniques, see Lombardo, M. M., & Eichinger, R. W. (2006).]

Interviewing for Potential: Learning From Experience Interviews

The discussion of learning agility in Chapter 3 dealt with a broad, general measurement of the characteristic. That approach is valid for making assessments of candidates' learning agility, but if you would like a more comprehensive measurement, there is an alternative.

Learning agility breaks down into four separate factors (Lombardo & Eichinger, 2000): Mental Agility, People Agility, Change Agility, and Results Agility.

Mental Agility is reflected in a desire to tackle challenging problems and identify root causes. Individuals high in Mental Agility are innately curious and enjoy problems that are novel and involve dealing with ambiguities.

People Agility involves the ability to respond flexibly to different social situations and interpersonal challenges. Individuals who possess People Agility have the capacity to understand themselves and their impact on others.

Change Agility requires experimentation and resourcefulness. Change agile individuals can develop a vision of where they want to go and help others understand and take part in creating something new.

Results Agility calls for courage and stamina when faced with challenging circumstances. Individuals who are high in Results Agility create high-performing teams with sustained drive to get things accomplished.

Each factor is evaluated using the questions and probes format discussed in Chapter 3. Separate ratings are made for each factor of learning agility. The ratings need to be evaluated as a whole. Even an individual with a high overall level of learning agility may show weakness on a particular factor. Likewise, some individuals may shine in just one area. Others will show consistency across-the-board. The potential impact of different patterns of results on job performance and future potential needs to be weighed.

Conducting a learning agility interview is a rigorous and time-consuming process and a bit more challenging than a regular competency-based interview. The interviewer must have an in-depth understanding of each factor of learning agility, how it differs from the other factors, and how to spot it in the interview. Along with ratings on each factor, the candidate's skill at learning input and learning output is evaluated.

Interviews for potential can be used for selection purposes and should be conducted separately from competency-based interviews. The results of the potential interview can shed light on the general assessments of learning agility made by other interviewers.

Learning agility interviews are more frequently used as part of succession planning efforts. The most learning agile individuals are generally placed in the upper echelons of the organization's high potential talent pool. The results of the interview can help determine which individuals possess the highest potential and what assignments will help nurture and maintain their learning agility.

Let's recap some of the things we know. We know that a structured, behavior-based interview process that focuses on competencies critical to job performance delivers superior results. With that in mind, our topics for additional focus deal mainly with how to optimize the structured interviewing process. We've selected five topics that deserve more attention:

(1) What Format(s) Should Be Used?

Face-to-face, one-on-one interviewing has always been a mainstay, but alternatives such as phone interviews and videoconference interviews have been explored more recently (Straus, Miles, & Levesque, 2001). The relative benefits and drawbacks of these approaches are still uncertain.

(2) Single Interviewers vs. Panel Interviewing

The merits of conducting a sequence of one-on-one interviews or a single panel interview have been heavily debated. A stated advantage of panel (more than one person) interviews is that inter-rater reliability (interviewers agreeing with one another) is higher because everyone hears the same questions and answers. Supporters of the single interviewer approach contend that validity (how accurate the interviewer assessment turns out to be over the long term) is higher because a broader sample of candidate behaviors is captured across the different interviews. Thus far, research has not declared a clear winner; each method has support (e.g., Huffcutt & Woehr, 1999; Wiesner & Cronshaw, 1988).

More might be learned by taking a closer look at the practical considerations of conducting each approach. Which approach is easier and more efficient? Scheduling several individuals to convene at one time or finding a number of separate occasions where the candidate can meet with an interviewer? Applicant reactions should also be taken into account. Which is of less concern to you? Is it candidate fatigue from participating in multiple one-on-one interviews or candidate stress from having to go through an interview with several people asking questions? A deciding factor in choosing between the two approaches may be which is more relevant to the job. In particular, the panel interview may be a preferable option when stress tolerance and dealing with multiple people simultaneously are important elements of the job. This may partly be the reason why panel interviews are commonly used in police and fire department selection systems. Panel interviewing has its own technology and best practices. Those are beyond the scope of this book.

(3) Establishing and Supporting the Structured Interview Process

Best practices are also needed to "roll out" structured interviewing practices in the organization. One recommendation we can make is to get familiar with the past interviewing practices in the organization. Then identify how much of a departure the structured approach represents from the way things have been done before. This will at least let you know what type of gap you need to bridge and how big it might be. Another suggestion would be to introduce the process gradually, perhaps pilot testing it in just one level and/or function in the organization.

The thing to keep in mind is that most untrained interviewers have informal, casual, minimally planned conversations. The approach we are outlining is a disciplined, structured, consistent, planned process. Personal preferences as an interviewer are not allowed. This is a science-based, structured conversation. Even motivated people looking to become better interviewers will struggle with the rigidity of this process.

Beyond that, the caveat appears to be whatever works best for your particular organization. Some of the approaches we have heard include getting initial buy-in from an influential group in the organization, applying the interview process either to high-volume or difficult-to-fill roles in order to demonstrate its effectiveness, establishing "power users" who will be advocates for using the process, and setting up "learning circles" to share experiences and insights from conducting structured interviews. Over time, it would be nice to get some clarity around these suggestions and determine which ones most consistently lead to success across different settings.

(4) Interviewer Training

Research suggests that interviewer training is beneficial and contributes positively to interviewing outcomes (e.g., Huffcutt & Woehr, 1999). We know that the elements of a good training program should include an introduction to the science behind interviewing, a review of best practices, and practice in applying interviewing techniques. Considerations that still need clarification include how long the training should last, whether a blended approach of technology-based and classroom instruction should be used, and what type of follow-up should be conducted. With regard to follow-up, the actual impact of training on interviewer behaviors should be measured both immediately and over time. Trends in the data might indicate when interviewers start to deviate from their training and fall back on old, more comfortable habits. This would signal an opportune time to engage individuals who have gone through training in a refresher course.

(5) Interviewer Expectations and Reactions

Critics of structured interviewing contend that, occasionally, interviewers will dislike the process because it restricts their freedom and requires more time and effort. While we feel these claims are not supportable in terms of the results you can achieve, it is necessary to identify and respond to concerns that interviewers might have about the process. You need to promote awareness of the benefits of structured interviewing practices. Some research has been done in this area. Attending a training workshop on structured interviewing does increase participants' buy-in to the structured interviewing process (Lievens & de Paepe, 2004). When individuals see the positive results that come from using the process, they will need less convincing.

CHAPTER 7

BECOMING A BETTER INTERVIEWER

Aside from learning, practicing, and perfecting the techniques and best practices of structured interviewing, there are additional developmental things you can do to become an even better interviewer.

Interviewing skills are developed and refined over the course of a lifetime. Knowing your strengths and weaknesses as an interviewer will aid your accuracy. So, you need an action plan for improvement.

One key to any improvement plan is to focus on the competencies that contribute to interviewer success. Interviewing is a complex process that draws off a number of skills. The table below shows a set of competencies that we see as relevant to performance and improvement as an interviewer at various stages of the process. Information about the competencies and how to apply them to the interview process is provided after the table. The numbers next to the competencies are the Lominger competency library numbers (out of 67).

Planning	Interviewing	Evaluating/Deciding
17. Decision Quality	2. Dealing with Ambiguity	2. Dealing with Ambiguity
25. Hiring and Staffing	3. Approachability	12. Conflict Management
46. Perspective	11. Composure	17. Decision Quality
47. Planning	12. Conflict Management	21. Managing Diversity
52. Process Management	31. Interpersonal Savvy	25. Hiring and Staffing
	32. Learning on the Fly	27. Informing
	33. Listening	33. Listening
	36. Motivating Others	37. Negotiating
	41. Patience	41. Patience
	45. Personal Learning	46. Perspective
	46. Perspective	51. Problem Solving
	56. Sizing Up People	52. Process Management
	62. Time Management	55. Self-Knowledge
		56. Sizing Up People
		57. Standing Alone
		64. Understanding Others

You might want to do a simple self-assessment to see what your strengths and development opportunities might be as you read the rest of this chapter.

Competency	Better than most people I know	About the same as most people I know	Could be a bit better	Probably an issue for me
2. Dealing with Ambiguity				
3. Approachability				
11. Composure				
12. Conflict Management				
17. Decision Quality				
21. Managing Diversity				
25. Hiring and Staffing				
27. Informing				
31. Interpersonal Savvy				
32. Learning on the Fly				
33. Listening				
36. Motivating Others				
37. Negotiating				
41. Patience				
45. Personal Learning				
46. Perspective				
47. Planning				
51. Problem Solving				
52. Process Management				
55. Self-Knowledge				
56. Sizing Up People				
57. Standing Alone				
62. Time Management				
64. Understanding Others				

Dealing with Ambiguity (#2). Interviewing and assessing people is an inherently fuzzy task. Structuring the process helps lessen ambiguity, but will not eliminate it completely. The interviewer needs to deal effectively with uncertainty and ambiguity and not get unnerved or slowed down by a lack of clear or complete information.

- **Interviewing:** Be patient and wait for information to emerge that will give you a better understanding of the candidate. The way to decrease uncertainty is by getting more information through asking and listening. Consistently following the structured probes will lead you to a better understanding of the candidate's actions and insights.

- **Evaluating/Deciding:** Look for patterns and themes in the candidate's answers to help fill in blanks and establish connections between seemingly unconnected pieces of information. Sharing information and perspectives with other interviewers during the evaluation stage also adds clarity. No one on the planet is capable of making perfect people decisions. Every interviewer will have an error rate. Try to make it as small as possible by considering all of the data you have collected and filling in the empty parts the best you can.

Approachability (#3). Structured interviews have a more formal tone, but that doesn't mean the interviewer should come across as cold or distant. The interviewer still needs to engage the candidate and set a tone that is conducive to conversation. If you don't appear confident in your role or interested in taking part, the candidate will pick up on your discomfort.

- **Interviewing:** Set rapport first. Think of a few things to say to initiate the interaction. Once you think the candidate is at ease, transition into your opening remarks and describe the interview process. Make sure the candidate has sufficient opportunity to ask questions. If the candidate appears unusually nervous, proceed calmly and smoothly; maintain a relaxed posture and be careful not to use a harsh or interrogating tone when asking questions. Some candidates like it when you begin a question by addressing them directly (e.g., "So, Greg, tell me about a time…"). A candidate who is at ease will disclose more information. An interviewer who is open and at ease will get more information.

Composure (#11). Things come up in an interview that will test your composure. Candidates will say things that will set you back, might be counter to your own belief system, or even make you upset or angry. As an interviewer, you really shouldn't react. Keep your cool.

- **Interviewing:** Act calm and polite, but maintain a neutral stance with your emotions. If you hear something that is particularly exciting or even something that grates on you, keep your reaction subdued. Often, immediately jotting some notes will help you keep some emotional distance and mask your reaction. Try doing some mock interviewing where the candidate tries to upset you, with a third party acting as an observer to tell you how well you are keeping your poker face.

Conflict Management (#12). There is conflict in all human exchange. Interviews are no exception. Sometimes a particular question will touch a nerve in a candidate that may either lead to a more aggressive response or a reluctance to divulge information. Many candidates will become defensive. Dealing with this conflict successfully or unsuccessfully can strongly influence the remainder of the interview and its eventual outcome. Conflicts may also occur following the interview when discussing the candidate with colleagues and making a decision.

- **Interviewing:** Conflict is natural. Watching a candidate in a conflict situation might even provide some useful information. The most successful way to manage natural conflict is through good preparation before the interview. Look for indicators on the candidate's resume—such as a job loss or poor performance of a business unit—that may come into play during the interview and may also provoke a negative response. Don't avoid these areas, but be prepared for how the candidate might react and how you will handle the situation. Conflicts, especially those involving unwillingness to respond to questions, often come about because of misunderstandings about the process and why the interview is being conducted. Scripting your remarks to the candidate to begin the interview and leaving ample opportunity for questions can promote mutual clarity and reduce candidate anxiety and concerns. Finally, when conflicts do occur, keep your composure. Engage your listening and patience skills to keep things from escalating, and maintain forward progress in your discussion with the candidate.

- **Evaluating/Deciding:** Conflicts can occur for many reasons during debriefing discussions on a candidate. They might include misunderstandings about what was said about the candidate, different perspectives on what is important, inherent biases in evaluating others, and personal agendas. Quickly identifying the underlying reason for the conflict is likely to be the key to resolving it as quickly and cleanly as possible. There is certainly value to letting a conflict play out and allowing different sides to make their case, just make sure that the conversation stays civil, focused, and pertinent to the matter at hand.

Decision Quality (#17). Obviously, a lot rides on the decisions you make regarding candidates. Many of the prescriptions in this book are aimed at helping you make better decisions. Still, mistakes will inevitably happen. The best way to improve your decisions moving forward is to take a close look at what went wrong. If you can spot flaws in your approach to preparing, gathering information, or evaluating results, try to find a remedy and a way to reinforce it during future interviews.

- **Planning:** One of the most critical decisions during the planning stage involves choosing which competencies to include in the interview. If you are in the position of making this choice or contributing to it, carefully consider the requirements of the position and the competencies that have differentiated superior performers from poor performers.

- **Evaluating/Deciding:** If a group is involved in making the decision, then everyone should participate in reviewing what happened and how future decisions could be improved. Over time, patterns often emerge. For instance, some companies come to the conclusion that their "maybe" candidates should really have been classified as "not qualified" and then adjust their future evaluations accordingly.

Managing Diversity (#21). Interviewing will invariably expose you to individuals with widely different backgrounds, experiences, skills, and personal traits. Quite often, the candidate's characteristics may differ significantly from your own. This can present challenges when it comes to understanding those differences and interpreting their impact. There can also be language problems if the candidate's lead language is not the same as yours.

- **Evaluating/Deciding:** The important takeaway is to avoid evaluating the candidate solely from the perspective of your own background, experiences, etc. It is also necessary to objectively evaluate what the candidate brings to the table as an individual and not as a member of a particular class, etc. When making note of differences of any kind, it is important to first determine if those differences are in any way meaningful to performance on the job. If so, both positive and negative implications should be explored as well as how they might be addressed in managing the individual. Always be careful of the presence of bias or stereotype in your perceptions.

Hiring and Staffing (#25). This is a broader issue that goes beyond just the interview. The pertinent questions here include, "Does our recruiting and selection system work the way we want it to? Does it produce expected results? Do we hire high-quality talent?" Answering these questions requires gathering multiple data points and looking at outcomes from several perspectives. The root causes for unmet expectations can be both systemic and personal. Maybe the overall success profile for people in the organization needs to be adjusted. Perhaps the definition for talent is too narrow and restrictive. Maybe a lack of courage exists to take a chance on candidates who don't fit the conventional mold and might emerge as change agents. Maybe you aren't looking in the right place. Whatever the outcome of your analysis, make sure the interview and other elements in the selection process are structured to capture the information you need.

- **Planning:** Make certain you have clearly and carefully defined the requirements for the job and the competencies needed to meet them. This way, you can structure the interview process around identifying the specific skills essential for success and not rely on feel or gut instincts to find a candidate with the right talents.

- **Evaluating/Deciding:** Always use the success profile for the job as a reference point in evaluating candidates' qualifications. This helps guard against drifting from the mark and either "settling" for a less-qualified candidate or gravitating toward a candidate with a set of skills that are impressive but not necessarily tied to overall success.

Informing (#27). The end result of the interview process is information. If you are participating with others in making a hiring decision on the candidate, it is important that you relay the information that you gathered in a timely, clear, and thorough manner to the people who need it.

- **Evaluating/Deciding:** Just as you should avoid winging it when you conduct the interview session, the same practice holds for post-interview discussions. The more time you take to pull together your thoughts and prepare your comments, the more efficiently and effectively (not to mention persuasively) you will be able to present your findings to others. A key here is to know your audience and how they like information presented to them. Do they prefer bullet point comments or more lengthy narrative overviews? Do you start with the conclusion or build up to your case? Do they want to hear the negatives first or the positives? Remember, it is not only the raw information you provide, but how you package it that makes a difference.

Interpersonal Savvy (#31). You will meet all kinds of people when interviewing candidates. Some will be easy to read and have very accessible personalities, and some will be rather closed or difficult to talk to. Either way, it's your job to make sure that the interaction flows reasonably smoothly and that the candidate has the opportunity to show his or her true capability. Pulling this off can sometimes require a bit of flexibility and finesse on your part.

- **Interviewing:** A good first impression is hard to make a second time. A good start is your responsibility. The first rule is to be ready for anything. The second rule is to be ready to respond accordingly. Consistently presenting yourself to candidates as professional, open, and engaged is the key. Good improv actors tend to work by reading and responding to their audience, not trying to force the action. Use the initial minutes of the session to get a good feel for the candidate's attitude, demeanor, and personal style. Adjust your own baseline approach accordingly to create a comfortable interaction and plant the seeds for a good rapport. Your responsibility is to put the candidate at ease whether you are at ease or not. The first three minutes sets the tone. After that, once the structured portion of the interview begins, you are in the driver's seat and have more control over the tone and tempo. A good start makes this all the easier.

Learning on the Fly (#32). As you progress through the interview, you will sometimes be surprised as to what you find out about the candidate and where the information you encounter will lead you. Efforts at trying to connect the dots prematurely or accept surface meanings will often rob you of critical pieces of information and insight that could broaden your understanding of the candidate. Following the structure of the process, but at the same time going with the flow and keeping an open mind to what you are hearing, will help you to extract more from the interview. You will need to adjust your thinking on the fly to meet the candidates where they are.

- **Interviewing:** Make an effort to stay nimble and fluid during the interview. Keep a mental tally of your thoughts and perceptions. As you encounter new information and insights over the course of the interview, compare them to what you have already heard and consider what it adds to your judgments. Ask yourself questions and pose hypotheses to keep yourself actively thinking about what the candidate is telling you about his or her skills. Pursue leads as they present themselves.

Listening (#33). Active listening is sometimes described as listening without bias. Listening with open ears requires not only focused attention, but a willingness to hear others out. Not jumping to conclusions and suspending judgment until you've heard the whole story are important to remember.

- **Interviewing:** Active listening has a significant external component. Eye contact should be steady, facial expressions should convey attentiveness, and posture should be poised but not stiff. Asking questions is a big part of listening. Tone of voice when asking questions should be firm and direct, but also indicate some interest in hearing what the candidate has to say. During responses, avoid interrupting (unless clearly necessary) and let the candidate's thought process unfold. Don't complete the candidate's sentences or thoughts. Untrained interviewers talk too much. Remember that when your mouth is open, your ears are closed.

- **Evaluating/Deciding:** During the information-sharing and decision-making discussions, varied pieces of information will be presented and multiple viewpoints and opinions will come into play. Understanding and synthesizing this information requires careful attention and a willingness to probe for clarity and insight. All should have the time to express their viewpoints. It's important, when it is not your turn, to close your mouth and listen.

Motivating Others (#36). One of your main tasks is to get people to talk. Talk a lot. Sometimes you'll get a candidate who is apprehensive about the process and wants to play it safe. On rarer occasions, you may get a candidate who is not very invested in the process and seems to be going through the motions. In both of these instances, you want to give them a compelling reason to speak.

- **Interviewing:** The key to motivating others to speak is to convey that you have a genuine interest in hearing them and understanding what they are all about. You may want to subtly craft this message into some of your initial rapport building and opening comments before beginning the structured portion of the interview. During the interview itself, the tone with which you ask questions and the attentiveness you give to the candidate's responses can open the door to a more robust conversation. Just the right amount of note taking also indicates that you are engaged. A good interviewer can always find a way to make the question that he or she has asked a hundred times sound like he/she is asking it for the very first time. Some people are naturally quiet and shy. It's your job to bring them out. Some people are prone toward yes and no answers. It's your job to get them talking more.

Negotiating (#37). It's rare that different parties involved in making a candidate decision arrive at the information-sharing and decision-making session with the same idea in mind. Battles have to be fought and sometimes concessions need to be made. Doing this with the appropriate balance of force and tact is necessary to both preserve working relationships and make sure that fair and appropriate decisions are being made.

- **Evaluating/Deciding:** Anticipate issues where you feel you may have a different point of view from your colleagues. Know what you are willing to bargain on and where you are reluctant to concede. Also, knowing your position relative to others and what you are responsible and accountable for in the process may either add or detract from your position accordingly. In a win/lose situation, either losing with dignity or allowing others to save face is generally the best practice.

Patience (#41). Effective interviewing requires patience, a quality seldom found in experienced managers. It would be nice if you could go with your gut instinct and curtail the interview after a short period, but the research shows that this can be a misguided practice. Not jumping to conclusions and taking the time to hear things out can have its rewards. If anything, it shows a courtesy and respect for the candidate that can promote comfort and openness—which generally leads you more quickly to the information that you are impatient to get! Remember, talk less, listen more.

- **Interviewing:** With a slow-talking or reflective candidate, the natural urge sets in to interject and keep the conversation moving along. In these situations, just concentrate on listening and waiting. Oftentimes the questions that are asked require deep and discriminating thought, so rushing the conversation may leave critical insights unearthed. One-third of the people you will interview over your career will be paced, reflective, and deliberate. To an impatient person, that translates to too slow. It's your job to get the information by matching the pace of the candidate.

- **Evaluating/Deciding:** Sharing and discussing perceptions of a candidate can sometimes be a slow-moving, tedious process. Remember the importance of the information you are gathering to making the final decision and stick with the process. In some cases, you may want to caution others against sharing redundant information if strong agreement already exists. Also, don't unnecessarily rush decisions by declaring the matter open-and-shut or seeking a quick vote; allow due process to take place.

Personal Learning (#45). As charming, intelligent, and well liked as you are, your own personal style might not always be a good fit for the candidate and may impact the interview. Be sensitive to when you are not having the impact you want on the candidate, and adjust your approach.

- **Interviewing:** If you get the sense that your style (tone, pace, intensity, posture, nonverbals, etc.) is not working, make small adjustments in whatever areas you feel may be necessary and monitor the impact. If you feel you are having some difficulty with consistently having comfortable and productive interviews, have a colleague sit in on your sessions and provide some constructive feedback. Also, remember that you might not necessarily be the direct cause of the candidate's discomfort. Candidates, particularly those out of a current job, often come in with a weight of issues on their backs and sometimes require a little special handling to get them into the discussion. It's your job to adjust to the candidate, not the other way around.

Perspective (#46). The practice of interviewing can easily be thought of as focusing in on the specific information needed to make a precise decision as to whether or not a candidate meets the requirements for a particular job. While focus and getting down to specifics are indeed important, looking outward and keeping the big picture firmly in mind throughout the process are just as critical.

- **Planning:** Tactics are important during the planning stage. At the same time, having a clear view as to why you are conducting the interview, what you hope to gain from the process, and how the information you gather will play a role in the final decision will help to steer your planning efforts on the right track. Even though your task is short-term, it's also necessary to have the long-term in mind.

- **Interviewing:** Your attention during the interview needs to be strong and focused enough to hone in on what the candidate is saying, but flexible enough to also take a step back and ask, "What did that really mean? How does it relate to other things I have heard? What was the impact? What are the implications for the role I am interviewing for?" Answering these questions requires going beyond the here and now to consider broader meanings: How does this fit with all of the other people I have interviewed? Do I know other people who have worked for the same company? Have I ever been in that situation before? How did I react to a bad boss? If this type of thinking is a challenge for you, try formulating some specific questions ahead of time that you can ask yourself during and/or after the interview.

- **Evaluating/Deciding:** Consider debriefing the interview with someone who has an ability to look at situations from a global perspective. What types of questions or critiques does this person offer? What does this tell you about how to look at the candidate's experiences? Also, during the information-sharing and decision-making sessions, urge yourself and others to consider what is being discussed from different perspectives so an overly narrow view of the candidate does not develop.

Planning (#47). The importance of this skill pretty much speaks for itself. The rigor with which the structured interview is carried out cannot take place without sufficient planning.

- **Planning:** Know well ahead of time the competencies you are going to interview for and why they are important to the job. Study their meanings carefully and know what to look for during the interview session. Leave sufficient time before the interview to get settled and after the interview to take stock of everything you have learned.

Problem Solving (#51). Strong analytical skills are necessary to clearly and coherently piece together all the information gathered by you and others involved in the decision-making process. Surface-level observations, untested assumptions, and fuzzy logic can all undermine the quality of the decision being made.

- **Evaluating/Deciding:** Always look for patterns and themes and draw others' attention to them. Also hone in on information that is contradictory, missing, or incomplete. Stimulate and challenge others' thinking by asking constructive questions. Summarize key points and the information that supports them. Where necessary, be willing to challenge conventional views and provide a contrary position.

Process Management (#52). Making the entire interview process a smooth one requires a good feel for aligning people, information, and activities. Interviewing and hiring don't just "happen"; there needs to be a process to guide the way.

- **Planning:** Take a moment to map out all of the steps that occur in your organization's recruiting and interviewing process. Also, break down the interview itself into all of its various pieces. Take a close look at what you have laid out. Are there too many or too few steps? Are things in the right order? Does information flow smoothly through the chain? Do the steps make sense to the candidate? Based on your answers to these and other questions, see how the process can be reworked for added clarity, efficiency, and reliability. Seek input from others and pilot test new ideas before launching them system-wide. Where do you fit in the steps? What role are you playing?

- **Evaluating/Deciding:** According to systems theory, society functions on a definable set of processes and systems, some visible, some not, that keeps the wheels in motion. A usually leads to B closely followed by C. Organizations are no different. Knowing the written and unwritten processes that drive what happens in organizations can help you to better interpret candidates' experiences and separate fact from fiction. When a candidate tells you about a failed reorganization effort (it turns out that 75% fail), an underperforming unit he/she managed, or a missed promotion, measure what you are hearing versus what you know about how these events typically happen and what forces tend to drive them. Compare the candidate's story to your own experience. What would you have done in that same circumstance? The same goes for events in the candidate's win column. Was the win real or was it a windfall? These comparisons will give you insight into the candidate's real role in the process and what that tells you about his or her ability to apply the competency in question.

Self-Knowledge (#55). The importance of recognizing personal biases that affect your perceptions has already been mentioned a number of times. You should also get familiar with the general characteristics of your thinking style and how they shape your judgments. Are you more detail oriented and analytical or more inclined to look at the big picture and pay attention to your broad impressions? Do you value rationality and firm principles, or do you gravitate toward compassion and consideration? How you respond may indicate a lot about what you do and don't attend to in evaluating candidates, as well as which parts of the process you excel at or struggle with. The other part of self-knowledge is calibration. If you know yourself, you will be better able to judge others.

- **Evaluating/Deciding:** Being self-aware helps with candidate evaluation. This is especially true for the competencies you are interviewing for. A self-aware interviewer should, at the very least, make the judgment that the candidate is "better than me, about the same as me, or worse than me" on this competency. After you make the decision, then you can ask yourself where you stand on that competency relative to the job requirements.

Sizing Up People (#56). This competency pretty much gets to the core of what the interview is about. If you have difficulties here, you may be able to compensate with some degree of listening skills and perspective, but you will still have your work cut out for you.

- **Interviewing:** A key to your development will be learning to better recognize differences in others and then understanding what difference those differences make. First, accept the premise that individuals do differ appreciably in their skills and characteristics. These differences may have real implications for job performance. Next, spend time studying the people you work with. Compare them and identify differences. Learn to recognize links between their preferences and behaviors and what types of outcomes they produce. Try to translate some of your new insights into observing candidates during the interviews. Continue to observe others and add to your knowledge of how people differ from one another.

74

- **Evaluating/Deciding:** Having a broad as well as detailed understanding of others is of great benefit when evaluating candidates. The more "data points" you can reference for a particular skill, the better you can determine where a particular individual falls along a continuum—from unskilled to overused. Your people-reading knowledge is also useful when sharing information about the candidate. The better you are able to articulate your perception of a candidate's strengths and weaknesses to others, the easier they can digest that information and make a clear judgment about the candidate. Similarly, you can leverage your understanding and insight to help others make sense of what they observed in the candidate.

Standing Alone (#57). When all is said and done, you may find yourself alone in your perceptions of a candidate. The tough part comes in deciding what to do next.

- **Evaluating/Deciding:** First, gauge the true difference between your perceptions and the perceptions of others. In the ambiguity that can accompany group decision making, sometimes parties can end up in "violent agreement" with one another. If you are of a different mind from others in the group, try to first see it from their perspective and understand how the difference may have come about. Next, weigh the importance and impact of making your point. If you choose to go forward, try to formulate your point in a way that will be clear and persuasive, but not alienate the rest of the group. Be prepared to take some heat. Also, have an exit strategy—know how long and how intensely you are willing to do battle before standing down. Stand your ground, clearly state your view and, more importantly, your evidence, and then compromise if necessary.

Time Management (#62). Maintaining the right tempo and managing the clock are important elements in a productive, smooth-flowing interview. Avoiding the extremes is important. Approaching the interview as a series of boxes to be checked off and rushing the candidate through the process will often result in gathering only surface-level observations and might provoke a negative response from the candidate. Likewise, allowing a candidate to ramble or focus disproportionate attention on particular issues may limit the scope of what you take away from the discussion. Also, running overtime can impact the schedules of other interviewers and raise the anxiety level of the candidate, especially if he or she is expecting to catch a flight back home.

- **Interviewing:** One of the simplest and most effective remedies is to keep a clock in easy view during the interview and discreetly make periodic checks on your progress. Best practice is a wall clock only you can see or a desk clock. Looking at your watch frequently is not constructive. Have a rough idea of where you want to be at different stages of the session so you can ratchet the tempo up or down accordingly. Good active-listening skills and an appropriate sense of urgency are critical for effective time management. If you run into particular roadblocks with either very brief or long-winded candidates, refer back to the tips offered in Chapter 3.

Understanding Others (#64). Our identities and the foundation for much of our thoughts and actions are wrapped up in the groups we form and join. One candidate you interview might walk in the door with group identities such as ex-military, Red Cross volunteer, Boy Scout leader, and CPA. (Not that you would ask what groups the candidate identifies with; let's just assume it comes out in his/her responses.) Another candidate for the same job may present a completely different set of identities. The importance of these group affiliations is not to use them as easy labels or stereotypical devices, but to use them as filters for trying to understand the principles, beliefs, and assumptions that individuals put into practice on the job. They may help to explain decisions and actions that, at first, seem unfamiliar or out of context.

- **Evaluating/Deciding:** As you listen to a candidate's responses during the interview, try to understand what the individual has done within the context of the groups he or she identifies with. Does the person's work as a literacy volunteer somehow inform his approach to developing employees? Does the individual's former career as a police officer shape the way she interprets and responds to conflicts? As with other pieces of information, look for patterns and themes and engage in theory testing to support your conclusions. If you feel that someone's group identities are indeed going to exert a strong influence on how he or she performs, weigh the extent that this is either good or bad. Remember, your organization represents a group as well. How will that group's mind-set and beliefs interact with and have an influence on the individual's core identities?

The list above is not meant to be exhaustive. Please consider your own profile of competencies and identify where improvements will contribute the most to boosting your expertise and effectiveness as an interviewer. As you move forward, evaluate your progress against your plan and continue to learn from your experiences as an interviewer.

EPILOGUE

As Ken sat down in his office chair, he let out a brief sigh and said, "I've got to tell you, Carl, I'm feeling all mixed up about my interview with Amy."

"What exactly do you mean by that?" Carl replied, a hint of concern in his voice.

"Well, if I were to go purely with my gut, I would say let's hire her. That being said, I can't honestly put my finger on much in the way of specifics to tell you what would make Amy a good fit for the role or what I would expect from her day-to-day performance on the job. On top of that, I know from past history that my instincts on a candidate haven't always been dead-on."

Carl probed further, "Was there anything at all that concerned you?"

"A few things, maybe, but it's the same story there. The specifics are a bit vague, and I would be hard-pressed to tell you whether or not they would represent a real problem or if I'm making a big deal out of nothing."

"Do you need some more time to think about things?" Carl asked.

"That's not really the issue," Ken said tersely, some frustration showing in his voice. "All I've got are these general impressions. I don't know that any more thinking on the matter is going to make them any clearer. I understand that you can't know everything about a candidate, but at this point I need something more solid to grasp on to so I can make a more informed decision."

"Yeah, I would hate to see you either hire her or take a pass at this point without really being too sure about how you feel," said Carl, in an uncharacteristically hushed tone. "What do you propose we do at this point?"

"I'd like to bring her back in and have another chat, but it can't be a repeat of this morning. I need to come up with a game plan to walk away with some insights that will lead me to the right decision."

"That's good," Carl responded, the boom returning to his voice. "I think I can help you out there. I won't go into all the details right now, but I've been studying up on some different approaches to interviewing, and I've learned more about a set of practices and techniques that can lead you to a much better result than just sitting down and having an open-ended conversation with the candidate."

"Really?" Ken replied, with equal parts interest and skepticism. "I'd like to know more about that. Hey, this doesn't involve asking any questions about trees or favorite colors or anything like that, does it?"

"You're kidding, right? No, it's nothing off-the-wall or even that difficult. However, I will have to spend some time getting you up-to-speed before you have another meeting with Amy. We'll also need to have a discussion about what you're really looking for in this role so you can better understand how to approach it in the interview. If you don't really know the behaviors that you're looking for, it won't matter what questions you ask."

Ken shifted in his seat. "Well, you've got my interest. I always thought that how I approached interviews was just the way it was supposed to be done. I guess it's never too late to try a different approach, especially if the one I've been using has been something of a mixed bag in terms of results."

"Well, I would be more than happy to help get you on a different path," Carl said, reassuringly. "And don't worry; you're not the only one in this boat. I'm working on an initiative right now to get more hiring managers some fresh training in interviewing. Do you have some time to begin talking tomorrow?"

"There's never really any time nowadays, but I can move some things around. How does lunch at 12:30 sound?"

"That's great. See you then. Don't worry, Ken, we'll get this figured out."

"Thanks, Carl. See you tomorrow. Bye."

Ken hung up the phone. He felt a little better. However, he could still feel the frustration and some of the anxiety that had built up prior to his conversation with Carl. Ken knew that no matter what approach Carl taught him, it wouldn't eliminate that feeling completely when it came to making hiring decisions. However, if it could make it less frequent and intense, that would be great with him.

Ken glanced at his computer screen and saw a long list of e-mails waiting for replies. It was already 5:45, and he knew that he would have to tackle that task before leaving for the day. First, though, he wanted to take some more time to think about the interview with Amy. He turned around to face the window. As he looked out over the grounds and at the cars streaming along the highway in the distance, he began to think about how he could have approached things differently.

REFERENCES

Andler, E. C. (1998). *The complete reference checking handbook.* New York: AMACOM.

Cable, D. M., & Judge, T. A. (1997). Interviewers' perceptions of person-organization fit and organizational selection decisions. *Journal of Applied Psychology, 82,* 546-561.

Campion, M. A., Palmer, D. K., & Campion, J. E. (1997). A review of structure in the selection interview. *Personnel Psychology, 50,* 655-702.

Connolly, J. A., & Viswesvaran, C. (2002, April). *Assessing the construct validity of a measure of learning agility.* A presentation at the Seventeenth Annual Conference of the Society for Industrial and Organizational Psychology, Toronto, Canada.

Conway, J. M., Jako, R. A., & Goodman, D. F. (1995). A meta-analysis of interrater and internal consistency reliability of selection interviews. *Journal of Applied Psychology, 80,* 565-579.

Corporate Leadership Council. (1998). *Employee selection tests.* Catalog No. 070-198-213. Washington, D.C.

Eichinger, R. W., Lombardo, M. M., & Stiber, A. (2005). *Broadband talent management: Paths to improvement.* Minneapolis, MN: Lominger International: A Korn/Ferry Company.

Equal Employment Opportunity Commission, Civil Service Commission, Department of Labor, & Department of Justice (1978). Adoption by four agencies of uniform guidelines on employee selection procedures. *Federal Register, 43* (166), 38290-38315.

Gilbert, D. T., & Malone, P. S. (1995). The correspondence bias. *Psychological Bulletin, 117,* 21-38.

Goleman, D. (1998). *Working with emotional intelligence.* New York: Bantam Books.

Huffcutt, A. I., & Arthur, W., Jr. (1994). Hunter and Hunter (1984) revisited: Interview validity for entry-level jobs. *Journal of Applied Psychology, 79,* 184-190.

Huffcutt, A. I., & Roth, P. L. (1998). Racial group differences in employment interview evaluations. *Journal of Applied Psychology, 83,* 179-189.

Huffcutt, A. I., & Woehr, D. J. (1999). Further analysis of employment interview validity: A quantitative evaluation of interview-related structuring methods. *Journal of Organizational Behavior, 20,* 549-560.

Hunter, J. E., & Hunter, R. F. (1984). Validity and utility of alternative predictors of job performance. *Psychological Bulletin, 96,* 72-98.

Jones, E. E., & Davis, K. E. (1965). From acts to dispositions: The attribution process in person perception. In L. Berkowitz (Ed.) *Advances in experimental social psychology* (Vol. 2). New York: Academic Press.

Jones, E. E., & Harris, V. A. (1967). The attribution of attitudes. *Journal of Experimental Social Psychology, 3,* 1-24.

Lievens, F., & de Paepe, A. (2004). An empirical investigation of interviewer-related factors that discourage the use of high structure interviews. *Journal of Organizational Behavior, 25,* 29-46.

Lombardo, M. M., & Eichinger, R. W. (1989). *Preventing derailment: What to do before it's too late.* Greensboro, NC: The Center for Creative Leadership.

Lombardo, M. M., & Eichinger, R. W. (2000). High potentials as high learners. *Human Resource Management, 39,* 321-330.

Lombardo, M. M., & Eichinger, R. W. (2004). *The LEADERSHIP ARCHITECT® sort card quick reference guide.* Minneapolis, MN: Lominger International: A Korn/Ferry Company.

Lombardo, M. M., & Eichinger, R. W. (2004). *The leadership machine* (3rd edition). Minneapolis, MN: Lominger International: A Korn/Ferry Company.

Lombardo, M. M., & Eichinger, R. W. (2006). *The INTERVIEW ARCHITECT® professional handbook user's manual.* Minneapolis, MN: Lominger International: A Korn/Ferry Company.

Lorenzo, R. V. (1984). Effects of assessorship on managers' proficiency in acquiring, evaluating, and communicating information about people. *Personnel Psychology, 37,* 617-634.

McDaniel, M. A., Whetzel, D. L., Schmidt, F. L., & Maurer, S. D. (1994). The validity of employment interviews: A comprehensive review and meta-analysis. *Journal of Applied Psychology, 79,* 599-616.

Middendorf, C. H., & Macan, T. H. (2002). Note-taking in the employment interview: Effects on recall and judgments. *Journal of Applied Psychology, 87*, 293-303.

Miller, J. W., & Rowe, P. M. (1967). Influence of favorable and unfavorable information upon assessment decisions. *Journal of Applied Psychology, 51*, 432-435.

Moscoso, S., & Salgado, J. F. (2004). Fairness reactions to personnel selection techniques in Spain and Portugal. *International Journal of Selection and Assessment, 12*, 187-196.

Muchinsky, P. M. (1979). The use of reference reports in personnel selection: A review and evaluation. *Journal of Occupational Psychology, 52*, 287-297.

Posthuma, R. A., Morgeson, F. P., & Campion, M. A. (2002). Beyond employment interview validity: A comprehensive narrative review of recent research and trends over time. *Personnel Psychology, 55*, 1-81.

Rosenberg, D. (2000). *A manager's guide to hiring the best person for every job.* New York: John Wiley & Sons, Inc.

Schmidt, F. L., & Hunter, J. E. (1998). The validity and utility of selection methods in personnel psychology: Practical and theoretical implications of 85 years of research findings. *Psychological Bulletin, 24*, 262-274.

Schneider, B. (1987). The people make the place. *Personnel Psychology, 40*, 437-453.

Schneider, W. E. (1994). *The reengineering alternative: A plan for making your current culture work.* New York: McGraw-Hill/Irwin.

Smither, J. W., Reilly, R. R., Millsap, R. E., Pearlman, K., & Stoffey, R. W. (1993). Applicant reactions to selection procedures. *Personnel Psychology, 46*, 49-76.

Springbett, B. M. (1958). Factors affecting the final decision in the employment interview. *Canadian Journal of Psychology, 12*, 13-22.

Straus, S. G., Miles, J. A., & Levesque, L. L. (2001). The effects of videoconference, telephone, and face-to-face media on interviewer and applicant judgments in employment interviews. *Journal of Management, 27*, 363-381.

Taylor, P. J., & Small, B. (2002). Asking applicants what they would do versus what they did do: A meta-analytic comparison of situational and past behavior employment interview questions. *Journal of Occupational and Organizational Psychology, 75*, 277-294.

Thorndike, E. L. (1920). A constant error in psychological ratings. *Journal of Applied Psychology, 4*, 25-29.

Tsai, W. C., Chen, C. C., & Chiu, S. F. (2005). Exploring boundaries of the effects of applicant impression management tactics in job interviews. *Journal of Management, 31*, 108-125.

Webster, E. C. (1964). *Decision making in the employment interview.* Montreal: Eagle.

Wexley, K. N., Yukl, G. A., Kovacs, S. Z., & Sanders, R. E. (1972). Importance of contrast effects in employment interviews. *Journal of Applied Psychology, 56*, 45-48.

Wiesner, W., & Cronshaw, S. (1988). A meta-analytic investigation of the impact of interview format and degree of structure on the validity of the employment interview. *Journal of Occupational Psychology, 61*, 275-290.

Williams, K. B., Radefeld, P. S., Binning, J. F., & Sudak, J. R. (1993). When job candidates are "hard-" versus "easy-to-get": Effects of candidate availability on employment decisions. *Journal of Applied Social Psychology, 23*, 169-198.

Williamson, L. G., Campion, J. E., Malos, S. B., Roehling, M. V., & Campion, M. A. (1997). Employment interview on trial: Linking interview structure with litigation outcomes. *Journal of Applied Psychology, 82*, 900-912.

Wright, P. M., Lichtenfels, P. A., & Pursell, E. D. (1989). The structured interview: Additional studies and a meta-analysis. *Journal of Occupational Psychology, 62*, 191-199.

ADDITIONAL RESOURCES

The best practices detailed in this book form the foundation for Lominger's INTERVIEW ARCHITECT® suite of products and other related interviewing tools.

The newest addition to our interviewing products is the *INTERVIEW ARCHITECT® Express Interviewer's Kit;* it features everything you need to conduct structured interviews in a compact, portable format. The *FastFlip* interview guide rests comfortably inside the accompanying portfolio and allows you to view competency definitions, questions, and behavioral indicators at a quick glance. The Interviewer's Kit also features a specially designed notepad that facilitates quick, accurate note taking and a unique Post-it™ pen for flagging key questions. The kit was designed to streamline your efforts in preparing for, conducting, and evaluating interviews so you can maximize your efficiency and effectiveness in hiring the best candidates.

The *INTERVIEW ARCHITECT® Professional Handbook* is your guide for practicing the 4D interviewing approach outlined in Chapter 5 of this book. For each competency, the *Professional Handbook* features dozens of questions separated into the four interviewing dimensions. Additional sections offer extensive information for helping to evaluate a candidate's strength in a particular competency. The depth and scope of the material provided in the handbook allows you to develop highly customized interviews and gain a detailed and nuanced understanding of how to use Lominger's competencies for selection purposes.

The *Learning From Experience™ (LFE) Interview Guide* allows you to assess an individual's level of learning agility using a structured interview approach. This is consistent with the approach described in Chapter 5 of this book. The *LFE Interview Guide* can be used for hiring and promotion decisions as well as for assessing your organization's bench strength by evaluating future potential. Similar in format to the *INTERVIEW ARCHITECT® Express* products, the *LFE Interview Guide* provides questions, structured probes, and behavioral indicators for assessing each of the four factors of learning agility.

For more information on these and other Lominger products, visit us at www.lominger.com.